MUSEUM THROUGH A LENS

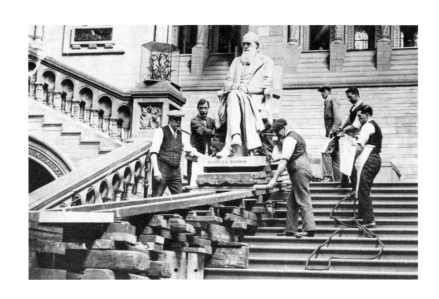

MUSEUM THROUGH A LENS

Photographs from the Natural History Museum 1880 to 1950

SUSAN SNELL & POLLY PARRY
FOREWORD BY DAVID BELLAMY

Published by the Natural History Museum, London

First published as *Life Through a Lens* in hardback, 2003
This updated paperback edition published by the Natural History Museum,
Cromwell Road, London SW7 5BD
© Natural History Museum, London, 2009
ISBN 978 0 565 09253 5

A catalogue record for this book is available from the British Library

Design by Mercer Design, London
Printed by C&C Offset Printing Co., Ltd, China

ASTRANGE AND WONDERFUL collection, that's what a museum should be all about and this book, the latest production from the 'world's greatest cathedral of natural history' lives up to those great expectations. Black and white they may be, but each photograph tells a story of the evolution of this institution from 1880 to the 1950s, by which time I had been a regular visitor for over twenty years.

An archive of ghostly facts waiting to be released from the glass plates and celluloid to enthral, entertain and educate families of a new millennium. Favourites, of course there must be. 'George' the elephant, so large that his ears got in the way of those great front doors en route to a makeover at the taxidermists. The *Diplodocus* that still greets you as you say 'Wow!' at the grandeur of the entrance hall. A fantastic £2000 investment even back in 1905, for it still brings the visitors in.

That these behemoths – and they looked much bigger when you were under ten – survived both incendiary and flying bombs is perhaps understandable; but the loss of plant specimens affixed to herbarium sheets by the then very rare female members of the Museum staff, was a real catastrophe of the Second World War. I can remember allotments in the Museum grounds, but I didn't know that the food they grew was fertilised by the skeletons of whales, amongst other things. A number of the pictures show that even through this more authoritarian time, staff of all ranks had a great sense of humour. The lucky ones also travelled the world in search of new specimens to put on show. No package holidays by plane in those early days, and no fridge to preserve the new material often shot by the upper echelons of the armed forces, both on active service and retired. Pickled in spirit and formalin, the work began in earnest on their return.

Even when as a student I was allowed to use the library, there were departmental tea clubs, as featured in these photographs. There you could gain refreshment and rub shoulders with the real practitioners of natural history. It was the finding of a volume entitled *The Peat Bogs of Polesie* that led me to a life immersed in the study of wetlands.

Like any museum, every book poses more questions than it answers. The following I have gleaned from its pages. Does the belly of the full-sized model of the blue whale really contain a time capsule, and if it does when will this Jonah be let out to tell its tale? Also, who was the audacious member of staff that appropriated the 'willy' of the marble statue of Adam which once stood over the entrance?

Now you can own this very special part of the Natural History Museum, and please, before you place it in your archives, live up to the aspirations of all great curators who have gone before. Mark this book with your name and the date you got it. If ever you decide to start a museum of your own give it an acquisition number. All in your best handwriting of course.

David Bellamy, Fiori di Campo, 2003

FOREWORD

INTRODUCTION

OLD PHOTOGRAPHS hold a deep fascination for many people. In today's visual society, images provide a direct route into the past in a way that cannot be achieved by text alone. They enable us to actually see people as they appeared – or wanted to appear – to their contemporaries, and to glimpse the places they saw every day. This volume contains a small sample of just over a hundred photographs selected from the 6000 or so images in the Museum's Archives. They show staff, visitors, exhibits, galleries, architecture and day-to-day work, captured by men and women with an eye for posterity. Some photographs were taken as an official record or for publication, others by the casual visitor or member of staff wanting to capture a fleeting moment. All provide us with the chance to step back in time for a short while – to see life through a lens, no less.

SEVENTY YEARS OF MUSEUM LIFE

Just as photography was becoming a popular and affordable recording medium, the natural history departments of the British Museum in Bloomsbury transferred to new, purpose-built premises in South Kensington. The Departments of Mineralogy, Geology (known as Palaeontology from 1956) and Botany took up residence first, and the Museum opened on Easter Monday 1881. It was a further two years before Zoology staff joined their colleagues and the collections were reunited in their new home, known familiarly (but not officially until 1992) as the Natural History Museum.

Unfortunately, no one seems to have recorded the construction of or move to the new building on camera, as no images survive of this vast undertaking among the photographs now preserved in the Archives. However, this book features a selection of many other images from this little known but invaluable photographic resource, dating from around 1880, when the Museum was nearing completion, until soon after the innovative Children's Centre opened some seventy years later.

These images, arranged chronologically, provide a visual record of the many changes that have occurred in the public galleries and behind the scenes. Of particular note is the transformation in the display and interpretation of natural history specimens. The earliest shots show regimented cases containing exhibits arranged by systematic classification, with little information besides scientific names. Over time, however, the galleries gradually began to change. By the 1890s the Central Hall featured realistic displays intended to show adaptation by animals, birds and insects to their surroundings, and elsewhere labels began to include information on geographical distribution and habitat.

Over the course of the 1920s and 1930s, this concept was extended with the creation of tableaux such as elephant and gorilla family groups, displayed in their natural surroundings in the Central Hall, and fossil fish dioramas in the Fossil Fish Gallery. Tremendous care was taken to ensure the inclusion of appropriate vegetation and background colouration for these remarkable new attractions. Plaster casts were used to represent some creatures that could not be shown as mounted specimens due to their soft tissues, and larger-than-life wax models of insects revealed details usually invisible to the naked eye. This trend to reveal all aspects of natural history to an eager public perhaps reached its artistic zenith in the construction of the blue whale model, the largest on display in the world at that time.

These pages record the increasingly-crowded galleries as the Museum strove to show visitors as much of the rapidly-expanding collections as possible. At the same time, there was ever more pressure on storage space for the research collections. By the mid-1930s the number of specimens had risen to almost 17 million – albeit still a fraction of the current 70 million. The Museum successfully lobbied for expansion space, gaining a new Spirit Building for the zoological specimens preserved in alcohol, and an Entomology Wing, the latter still under construction as the last images in this book were taken.

Brief biographical details in some of the captions reveal that both scientists and junior staff took part in expeditions to exotic locations such as South Georgia and the Canary Islands, to carry out research in the field and augment the Museum's collections. Such trips probably permitted some blurring of the strict delineations of scientific staff grades, ranging from Keeper, Assistant Keeper, 1st and 2nd Class Assistants to Attendants and Preparators. Some changes to titles occurred in the 1920s before all

grades were subsumed into Scientific Civil Service scales after the Second World War, becoming Scientific Officers, Assistants (Scientific) and Experimental Officers. It was also during the 1920s that women began to be appointed in significant numbers to the permanent scientific staff, and their arrival sparked a number of weddings. Many had been employed as 'unofficial workers', for important but poorly-remunerated tasks, whose service did not count towards a pension.

Some of the minutiae of daily life at the Museum are revealed through various images in this selection. Robert Bunting's informal shots capture the tradition of taking tea – many departments still operate 'tea rooms' today. Up until the early 1980s, staff had to collect their assigned key each morning from the Key Pound, just inside the main entrance. It was in this context that colleagues gently teased the wartime Salvage Officer for his conscientiousness in collecting scrap metal. These and other pictures, such as the staff dance of 1927, provide a glimpse of the morale-boosting humour that prevailed among staff, despite restrictive economic or wartime conditions.

Developments in fashion over seven decades can also be traced through the pages of this book. Facial hair, including full beards, seems to have been de rigueur for many male staff until about 1900 when various styles of moustache came into vogue. It is interesting to observe the changing styles in work wear, beginning with the very formal frock coats and top hats of senior staff, and the messengers' blue

'Windsor' uniform, embellished with red, originally granted to the British Museum by William IV in 1837. In contrast, the styles of the 1920s and 1930s are more relaxed, yet still formal in comparison to contemporary fashions.

PHOTOGRAPHY AND THE PHOTOGRAPHS

In addition to documenting a wide cross-section of Museum life, the images also give an insight into their photographers and changing techniques of photography. Frederick York, responsible for the first image in this book, probably used dry plate glass negatives that were in general manufacture from 1878 for his formal architectural shots. It is just possible that Robert Bunting might have used the new Kodak Brownie camera, available from around 1900, to take the light-hearted pictures of his Botany colleagues. A few years later the well-regarded photographer Benjamin Stone captured more formal staff groups, along with the okapi and other specimens. A Member of Parliament for fourteen years, it is said that as a backbencher "the only scenes he was responsible for were those reflected by his camera".

The rise of popular photography is reflected in the increasing number of photographs taken by visitors, including several women, by the turn of the 19th century. Some examples of these are included here, alongside images produced by commercial enterprises such as WHSmith and Raphael Tuck for stereoscopic cards and postcards of Museum highlights. By the mid-1930s, the development of Rolleiflex and other reflex cameras made it possible to record the work of the Museum in a more naturalistic style for the new photo-reportage magazines.

The core of the Museum's photographic archive comprises images pasted into three large red albums, but many other loose items have arrived in the Archives as part of departmental record transfers, or donated by or copied from former members of staff. Occasionally, the Archives have purchased photographs to add to the collection, such as a souvenir album of the old natural history galleries at the British Museum which includes four images of the new museum at South Kensington, taken around 1880 by Frederick York.

The photographs in this book reflect both the changes and enduring features of seventy years of life here at the Museum, while subject matter ranges in scope from world war to a genial afternoon cup of tea. There are of course many images that have not been included, and many more aspects of Museum life that were never captured by the photographer's lens. But this small selection of photographs, accompanied by the stories behind them, provides a tantalising insight into how things used to be, of life in all its forms at the Natural History Museum.

Susan Snell and Polly Parry
2003

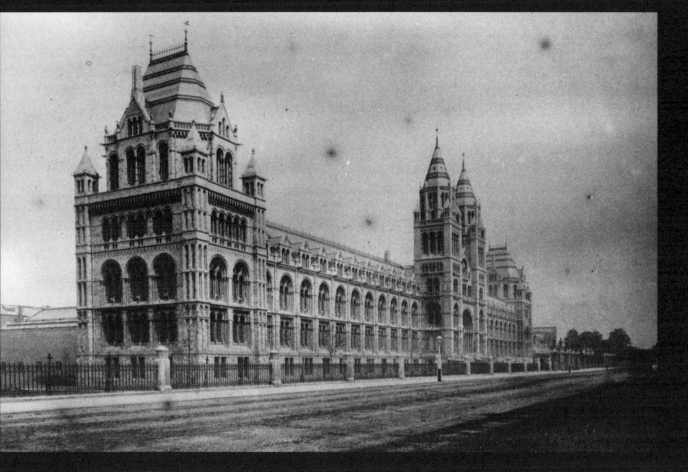

MUSEUM FROM CROMWELL ROAD, C. 1880

South Kensington had developed from rural estates, but by 1880 still remained on the western fringes of London. Its affordable land provided ample room for the construction of the new natural history museum. This advantage outweighed fears that it was too far from the centre of town for people to visit easily, despite the fact that an underground station had opened in 1868. After the Great Exhibition of 1851, land between Cromwell Road and Hyde Park had been set aside to create a centre for science and arts. The 1862 International Exhibition building was demolished to make way for the Museum, whose foundation stone was laid in 1873.

MUSEUM FROM CROMWELL ROAD, 1881
AND CLOSE-UP OF STATUE, 1920S

A statue, commonly assumed to be Adam, originally stood at the apex of the main entrance. It was initially unpopular due to the connection with creation rather than evolution, and the Victorian distaste of nudity. In 1940, the upper part of the statue smashed on the front steps, and the remnants were crated up and stored in the colonnade at the back of the Museum for the rest of the war. It was from here that the crates mysteriously disappeared and have not been seen since, although it is rumoured that the most notorious part of Adam's anatomy was used as a paperweight by a member of staff at the Museum.

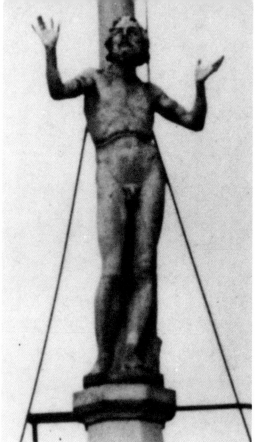

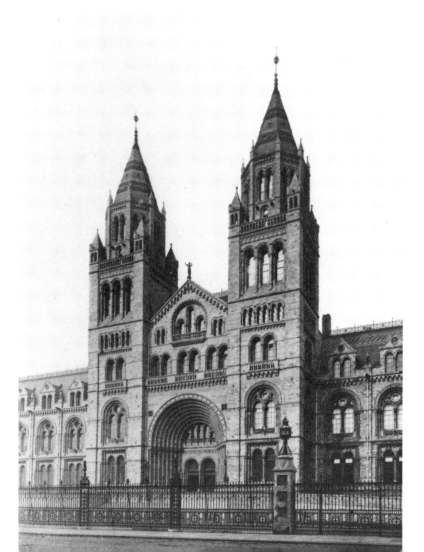

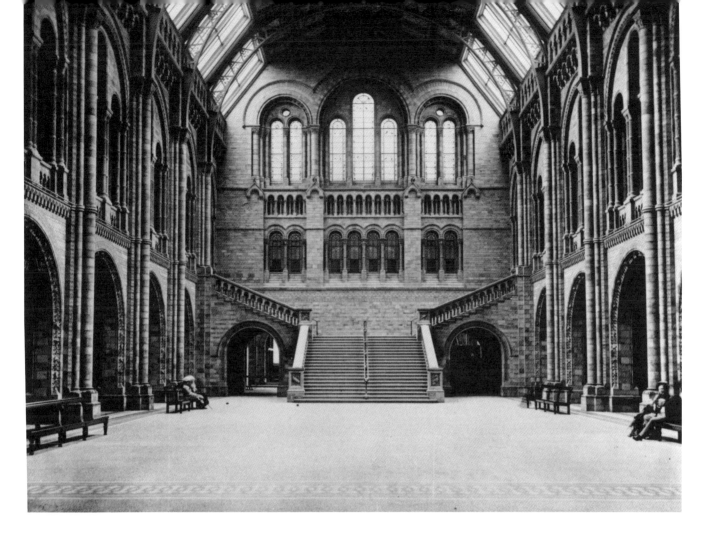

CENTRAL HALL, 1882

The Central Hall remained empty for about a year after the Museum opened, before a sperm whale skeleton was installed shortly after this picture was taken (see pp. 28–29). The cathedral-like space was described by one journalist in April 1881 as "a noble lofty hall…admirably lighted from above". New display cases, designed by the architect, Alfred Waterhouse, had to be specially built to fit into the exhibition galleries. This caused delays in moving the collections from Bloomsbury, so when the doors opened to the public on 18 April 1881, only mineralogy, geology and botany specimens were on display. The zoological collections did not complete their move until 1883.

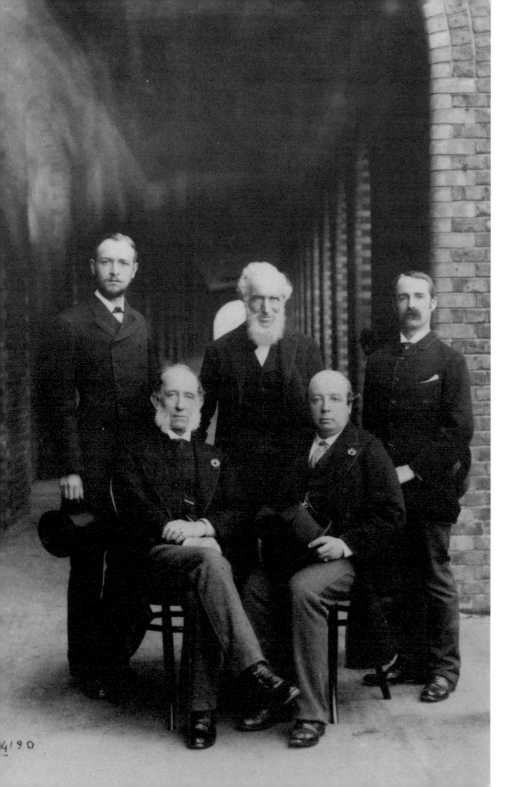

Senior Geology staff, 1885

In 1885 a series of staff photographs were taken in the colonnade at the back of the Museum. These gentlemen are senior staff from the Geology Department, including the Keeper, Henry Woodward (seated right) who started a popular series of guides to the exhibits. Arthur Smith Woodward (standing left, no relation) was appointed the next Keeper of Geology in 1901. He became involved with the discovery of the Piltdown skull in 1912, which appeared to reveal the existence of an entirely new early human species. In 1953 it was proved to be a forgery, created from a human cranium and a modern ape jawbone.

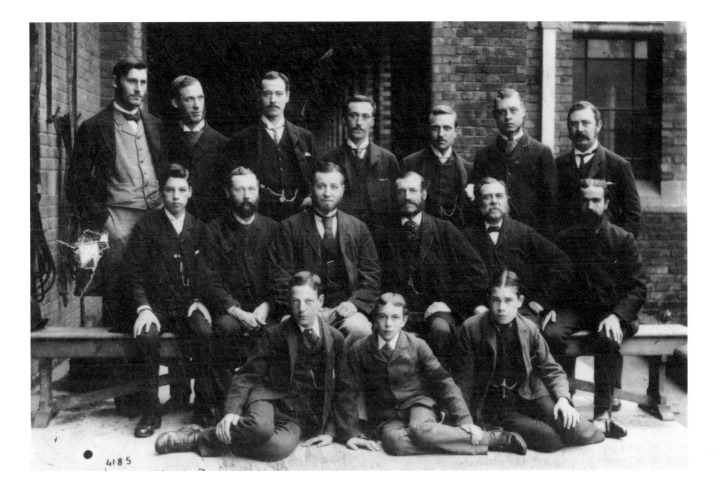

Junior Zoology staff, 1885

These are some of the more junior members – assistants and attendants – of the Zoology Department in 1885. Each department employed one or more boy attendants – four can be seen here (Walter Sarson on the left of the bench, Frederick Lowe, Charles Pratt and Thomas Wells in front). Most started aged fourteen, and were eligible for promotion to a permanent position as 'Attendant' once they reached eighteen. Their role was to assist the scientific staff, but a bright boy could certainly advance beyond menial tasks like cleaning, to mounting and labelling specimens for exhibition, registering new specimens, and clerical work such as copying out letters.

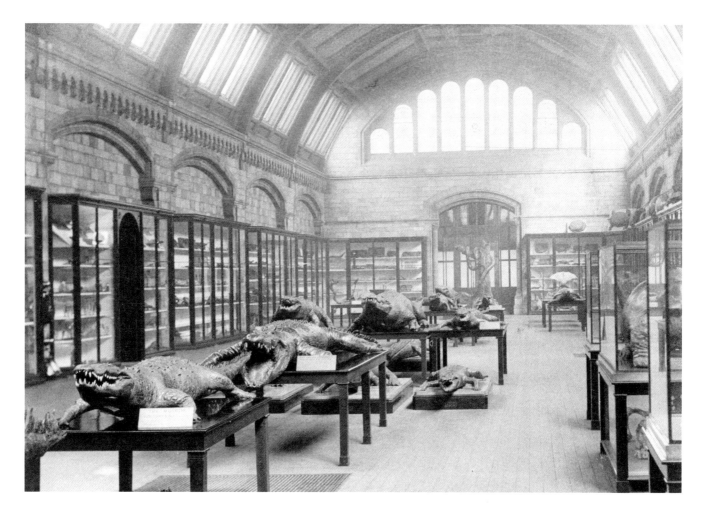

REPTILE GALLERY, NOVEMBER 1889

When this image was taken in 1889, the Museum's guidebook informed visitors that the Reptile Gallery displayed a "collection of stuffed specimens and skeletons of Reptiles, including Crocodiles, Lizards, Snakes and Tortoises". Victorians must have found the sheer size of these predators, once worshipped by the ancient Egyptians, an alarming spectacle. The fate of the mugger crocodile in the foreground, now an endangered species across Asia, seems at perilous risk from the jaws of the larger Indian crocodile behind. This mugger crocodile, some 9 m (30 ft) in length, was captured in north-east Australia.

Fish Gallery, September 1890

Several displays were not ready for the public until September 1885, four years after the building's official opening. Occupying "one of the elegant top-lit compartments in the North-West of the Museum", the Fish Gallery attractions included a 8.5 m (28 ft) long basking shark (middle of the picture) caught near Shanklin, Isle of Wight, and wood from a whaling ship, the *Farquharson*, pierced by swordfish lances. Perhaps to modern eyes this room appears a dry, gloomy aquarium, but one contemporary journalist praised the two sawfish from tropical seas and other specimens mounted on "telescopic stands effective for the display of denizens of the sea".

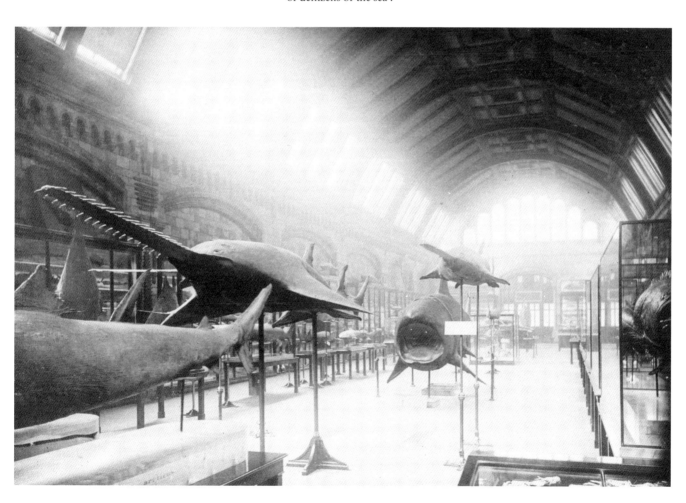

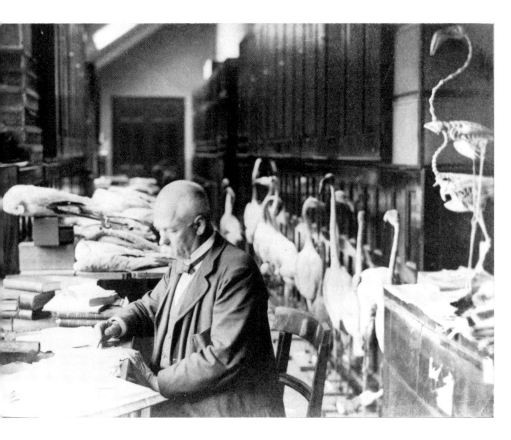

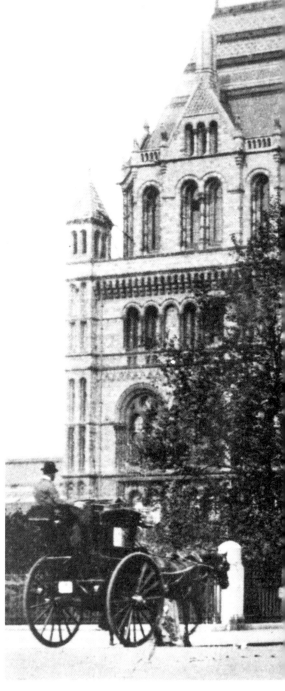

Tommaso Salvadori working on flamingoes, c. 1890

Museum staff have always collaborated with scientists around the world. Tommaso Salvadori, full title Count Adelaro Tommaso Salvadori Paleotti (1835–1923), was one of ten eminent ornithologists who assisted Richard Bowdler Sharpe, Head of the Bird Section, in preparing the 27 volume series, *Catalogue of Birds in the British Museum.* Responsible for three of those volumes, Salvadori is shown checking flamingoes in the Egg Corridor during his stay at the Museum between 1889 and 1891. Although his mother and his wife Bertha King were English, Salvadori returned to Italy where he was Vice-Director at the Museum of Zoology, University of Turin.

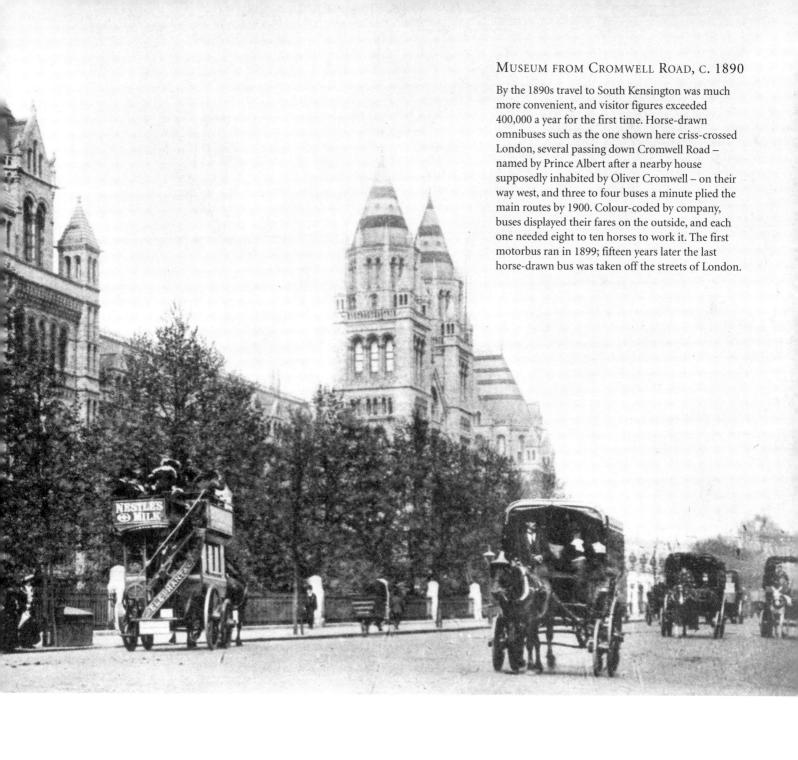

MUSEUM FROM CROMWELL ROAD, c. 1890

By the 1890s travel to South Kensington was much
more convenient, and visitor figures exceeded
400,000 a year for the first time. Horse-drawn
omnibuses such as the one shown here criss-crossed
London, several passing down Cromwell Road –
named by Prince Albert after a nearby house
supposedly inhabited by Oliver Cromwell – on their
way west, and three to four buses a minute plied the
main routes by 1900. Colour-coded by company,
buses displayed their fares on the outside, and each
one needed eight to ten horses to work it. The first
motorbus ran in 1899; fifteen years later the last
horse-drawn bus was taken off the streets of London.

OSTEOLOGICAL GALLERY, JULY 1892

Located on the second floor of the Museum, the Osteological Gallery was designed to show the visitor variations in mammalian bone structure. Larger specimens, such as the buffalo and bison shown here in 1892, were displayed in the centre and appear to march towards the door, while examples of ibex, eland and kudu horns (visible here), and other antelope, oxen and sheep horns adorned the walls above bespoke display cases. Skeletons of deer and rhinoceroses form the rearguard of this column.

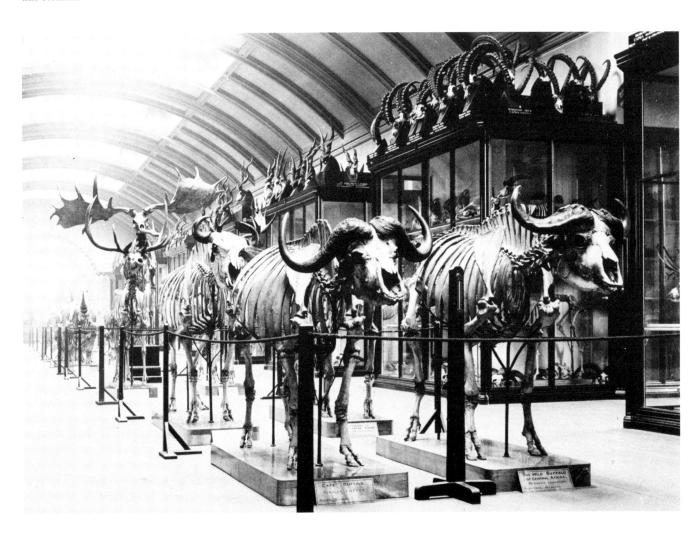

GIANT DEER, FEBRUARY 1893

Photographed by J.D. Pemberton in February 1893, this *Megalocerus giganteus* skeleton represents an extinct type of giant deer (also known as the Irish elk) that had a distribution throughout Europe, North Asia and North Africa. This example, presented to the Museum by William Willoughby, 3rd Earl of Enniskillen in 1883, was found in the shell-marl layer beneath peat bogs in Armagh, Ireland and has extremely large antlers with a 3.5 m (11 ft) width span. Carbon dates for some Isle of Man specimens revealed that this species survived until fairly recently, some 7000 to 8000 years ago.

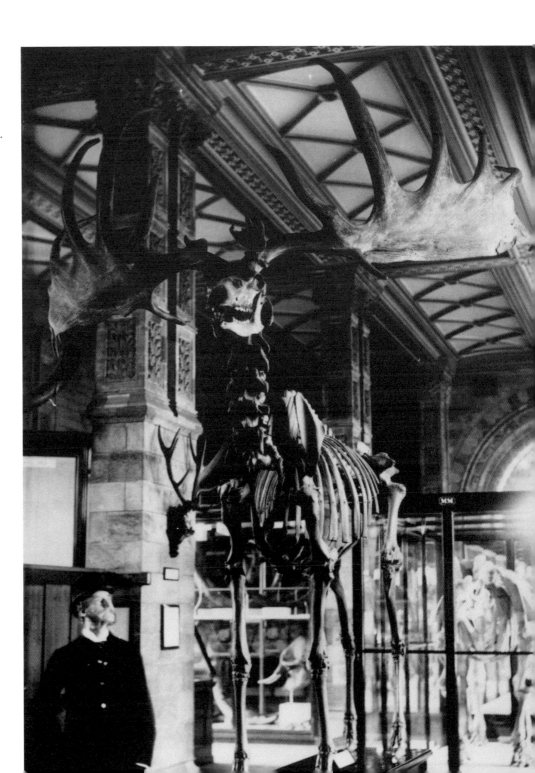

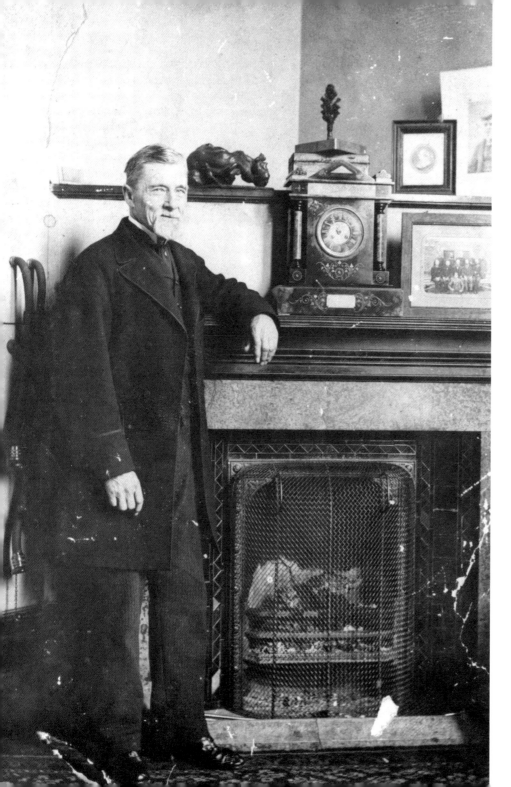

ALFRED CLAYTON, BOTANY ATTENDANT, C. 1894

This portrait of Alfred Clayton, who joined the Museum's staff in February 1858, was taken to commemorate his retirement in July 1894. His annual starting salary was £60 but this had doubled after 36 years' service, following his promotion from 2nd to 1st Class Attendant. Described as a "diligent, attentive and faithful servant" by William Carruthers, Keeper of Botany, Alfred was awarded an annual pension of £74 11s 11d. Coal fires heated some rooms, such as this Keeper's office, while other areas depended on inefficient radiators serviced by massive boilers. The photograph of Botany staff on the mantelpiece has also survived in the Museum's Archives.

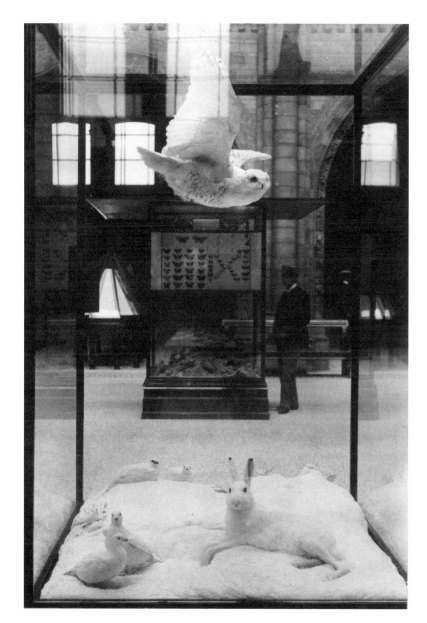

ANIMALS IN WINTER PLUMAGE, NOVEMBER 1897

A new series of display cases showing adaptation to surroundings in the natural world were unveiled in the Central Hall during September 1891. This case, one of a pair showing seasonal plumage, included a mountain hare, ptarmigan and willow grouse relaxing on realistic snow-covered heather, while a curious weasel observed the scene from a corner and a snowy owl flew overhead. All the specimens were presented by Professor Robert Collett from the University Museum in Christiania, (Oslo), Norway, to enhance the northern European collections.

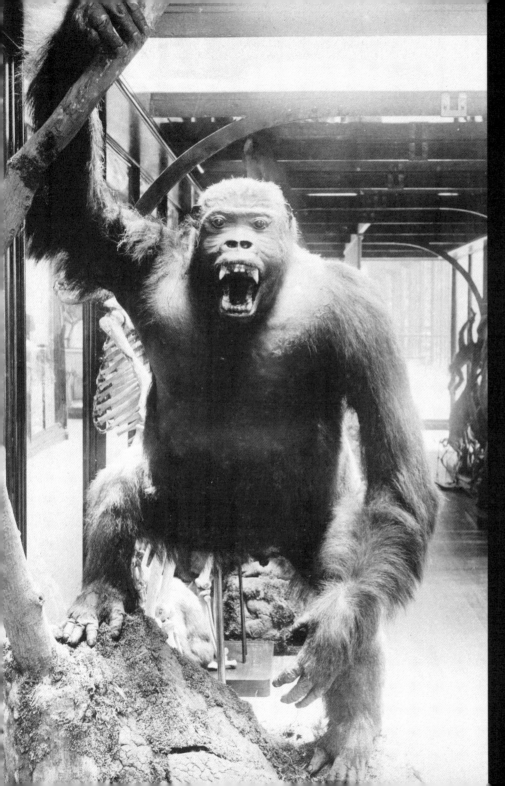

GORILLA, NOVEMBER 1897

As soon as Sir William Henry Flower replaced Richard Owen as Director in 1884, he commenced the gradual modernisation of Museum displays, introducing specimen labels containing information on geographical distribution and habitat. Under his new scheme, specimens from the Mammal and Osteological Galleries in the west wing were amalgamated to show skeletons alongside mounted specimens. The gorilla shown here in an aggressive posture became a popular Museum highlight. Epitomised in the 1933 film, *King Kong*, sensationalist reports by Paul du Chaillu and other early explorers strongly influenced the way in which these gentle giants were displayed.

INDIAN ELEPHANT, C. 1898

Jung Pasha or Jung Pershad was one of four Asian elephants brought back to London Zoo by Bertie, Prince of Wales (the future King Edward VII) following his tour of India during 1875–76. About five years old on arrival, Jung Pershad spent twenty years at Regent's Park, a firm favourite among the thousands of children given rides on his back. After his death from peritonitis in March 1896, taxidermist Edward Gerrard put his hide on display in the Central Hall. Other famous Zoo animals to find a permanent home at the Museum include 'Brutus the Lion', 'Guy the Gorilla' and 'Chi-Chi the Giant Panda'.

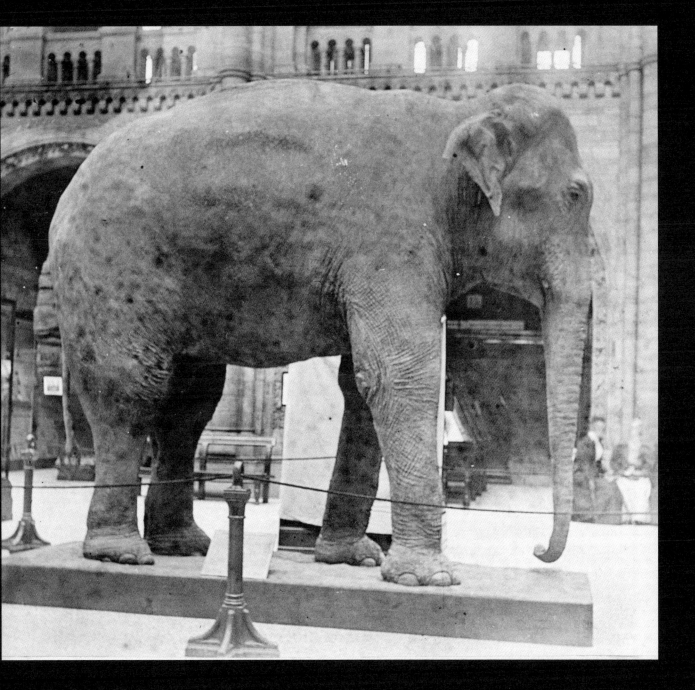

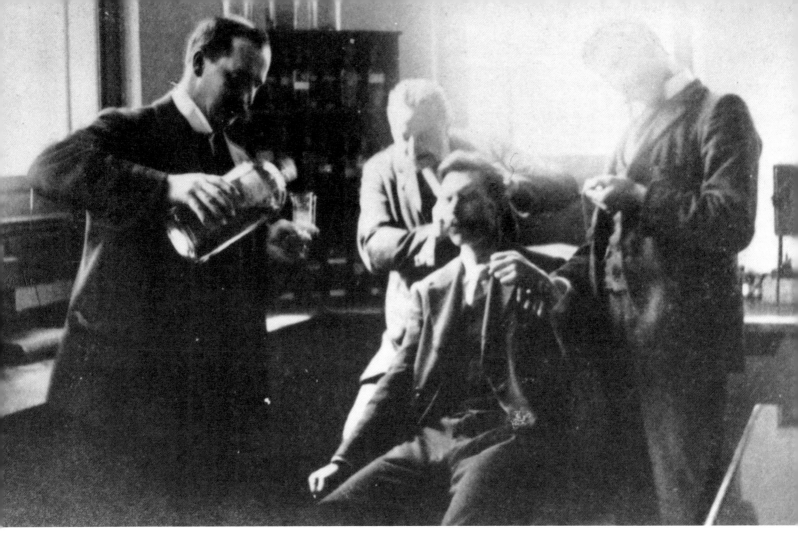

SCIENTISTS AT PLAY, 1899

An attendant in the Botany Department, Robert Hugh Bunting captured his colleagues at play in this humorous private photograph of Museum life taken in 1899. H.J. Badcock is the patient having his pulse taken in this tableau, while James Ladbrook administers a dose of alcohol, Herbert George Herring takes his pulse and William Robert Carver examines his head. Unfortunately the story behind this scene is lost – perhaps Badcock had just announced his engagement. Interested in amateur photography, 'Kipper' Herring, from the Zoology Department's Insect Section, later became the Museum's first official photographer.

WORKS STAFF OUTING, C. 1900

Turned out in Sunday best with fancy buttonholes, this group of 'Works' staff set off on an outing from Exhibition Road, c. 1900. William Cubitt and Co., who were contracted by the Museum in 1880, employed these housemen, painters, polishers and carpenters. Creators of the fine mahogany display cases, Cubitt staff transferred to the government's Office of Works when it became a Ministry in 1940. Perhaps the banjo and cornet were brought along to play *The Four-Horse Charabanc*, a popular music hall song of this period. Seeking fame and fortune, the photographer, Byng Inglis, moved his Bristol-based studio to nearby Chelsea in 1897.

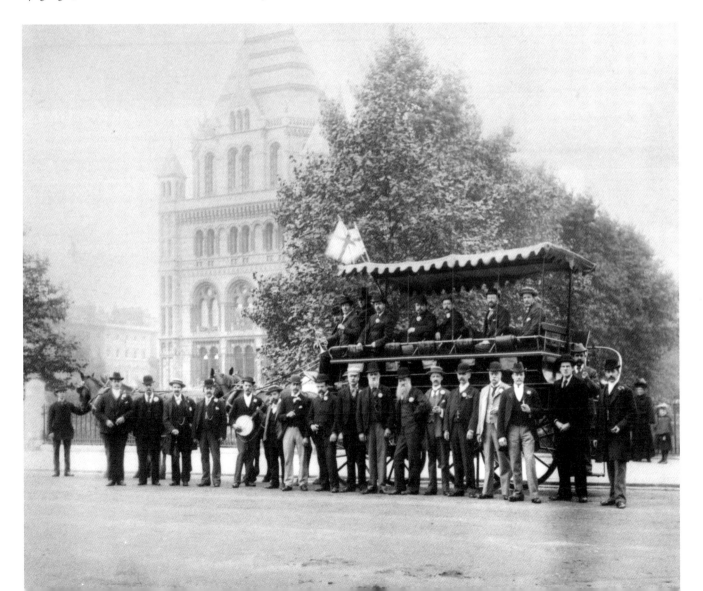

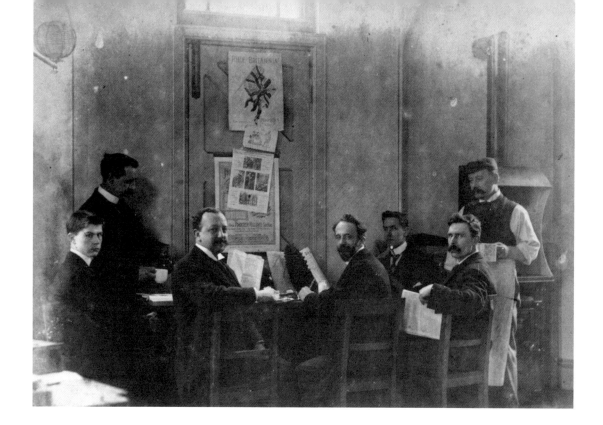

Botany staff, March 1900

Robert Hugh Bunting also photographed his
colleagues in a relaxed mood during March 1900.
While sandwiches are eaten, tea poured and
newspapers read, the patriotic poster on the door
serves as a reminder of the ongoing Boer War
campaign. The mantle protruding from the wall
proves that many parts of the Museum were still gas-
lit, and the heat came from a pot-bellied stove in the
corner. After sixteen years at the Museum, Robert left
in 1910 to work in Africa. He retained his interest in
natural history and sent the Museum plants and small
mammals from Ghana, Liberia and Sierra Leone.

Geology support staff, c. 1901

The identity of this group of characters on the front
steps of the Museum remains uncertain. It is believed
to include Geology Department support staff c. 1901,
exhibiting a variety of facial hairstyles and headgear
including caps, town shells, top and Coke hats. The
latter began life during the 1851 Great Exhibition when
James and George Lock of St James Street designed
a hat for William Coke, the future Earl of Leicester.
It was later manufactured by Thomas and William
Bowler and became known as a Bowler hat. Locks
still refer to them as Coke hats, and this headgear
remained a popular male accessory until the 1960s.

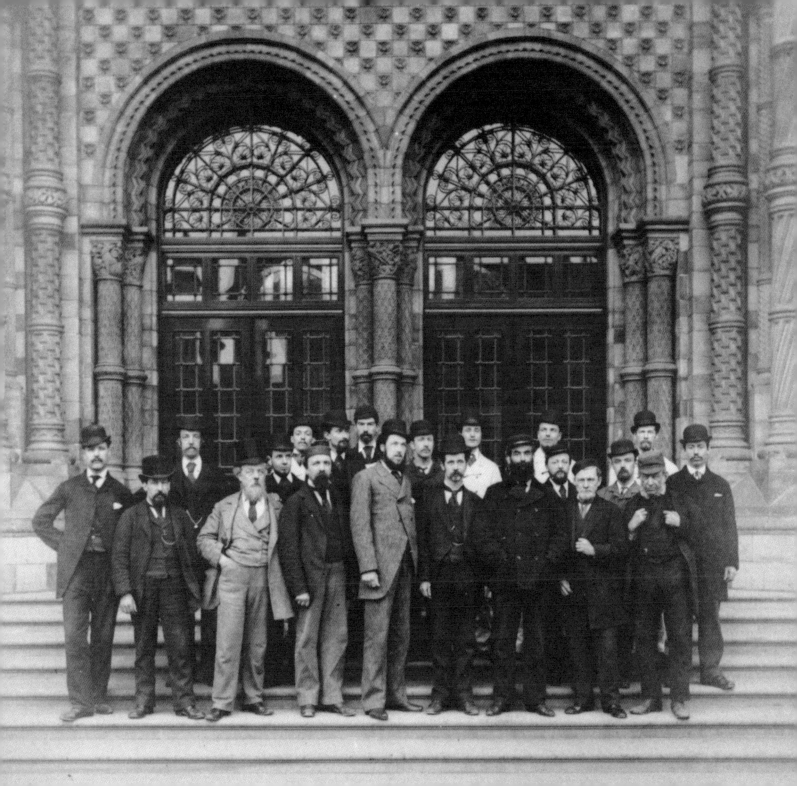

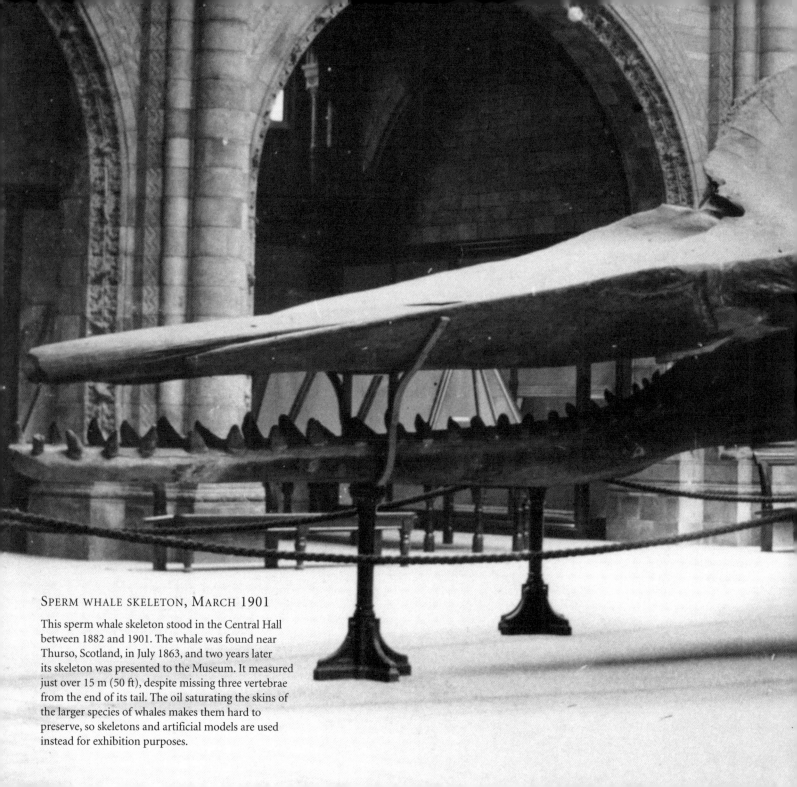

Sperm whale skeleton, March 1901

This sperm whale skeleton stood in the Central Hall between 1882 and 1901. The whale was found near Thurso, Scotland, in July 1863, and two years later its skeleton was presented to the Museum. It measured just over 15 m (50 ft), despite missing three vertebrae from the end of its tail. The oil saturating the skins of the larger species of whales makes them hard to preserve, so skeletons and artificial models are used instead for exhibition purposes.

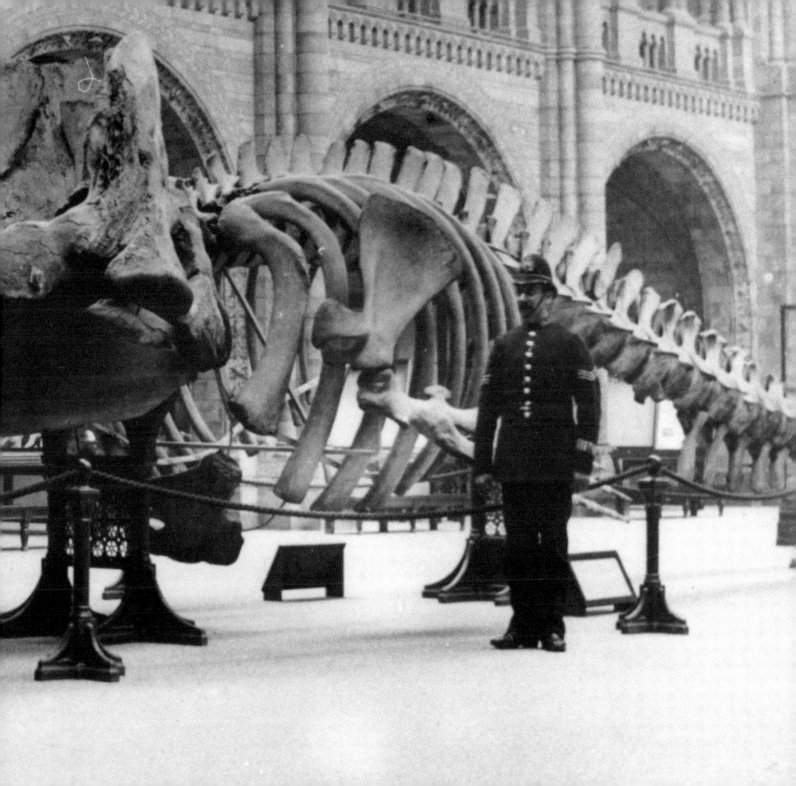

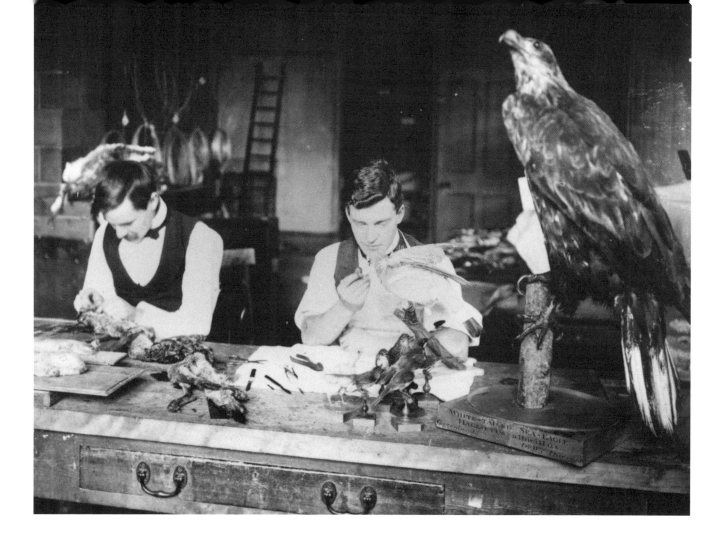

TAXIDERMISTS AT WORK, 1902

William Sherrin and Carl Seimund are shown here in their taxidermists' workshop in 1902. By the early 20th century, taxidermists were attempting to display specimens in lifelike poses, rather than the crude, caricatured style of hunting trophies that had been popular in the past. Seimund had fought in the Imperial Yeomanry in South Africa during the Second Boer War, returning home in 1901. Despite being on military service, he found time to help the officer in charge of the Yeomanry Hospital in Deelfontein, Colonel Arthur Sloggett, to collect 316 mammals and 1054 birds, eggs and skeletons from the Cape Colony which were sent back to the Museum.

Giraffes on steps, October 1903

Following the redevelopment of the Upper and Lower
Mammal Galleries in 1898, more space was needed to
exhibit larger animals to an eager public fascinated by
discoveries made on worldwide expeditions. This trio
formed part of the new mammal display in 1903
along the first floor east and west corridors. Due to
their size, finding storage and exhibition space for
giraffes continues to be a challenge. By coincidence,
giraffes were located near a staircase at the British
Museum before the move to South Kensington and
their former home in the Museum's basement is still
known to staff as Giraffe Corner.

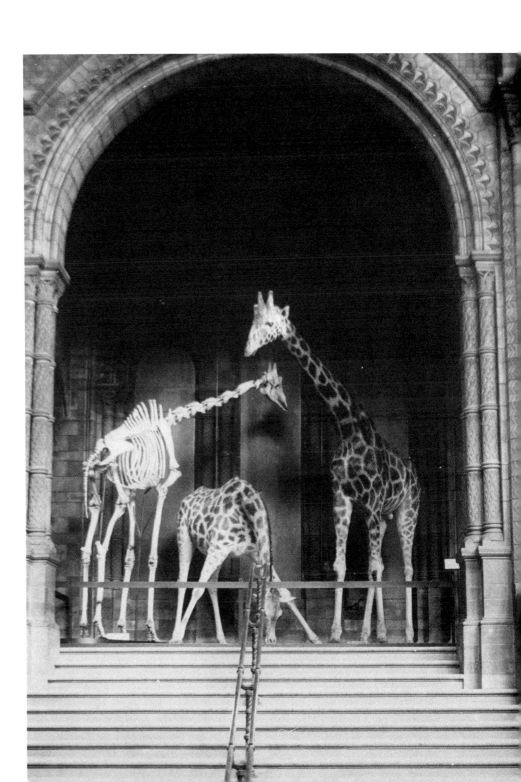

PRESENTATION OF DIPLODOCUS, MAY 1905

Arguably the Museum's most famous exhibit, the cast of *Diplodocus carnegii* was presented by the Scottish-American industrialist Andrew Carnegie. The original skeleton, excavated in Wyoming, is in the Carnegie Museum of Natural History, Pittsburgh, USA. In 1903, after the interest shown by King Edward VII, Carnegie offered to have a cast of *Diplodocus* made, at his own expense (about £2000), for the Museum. The official presentation ceremony took place on 12 May 1905, and Lord Avebury, one of the Trustees, is shown here accepting the gift from Carnegie on behalf of the Museum, before an audience of around 300 people.

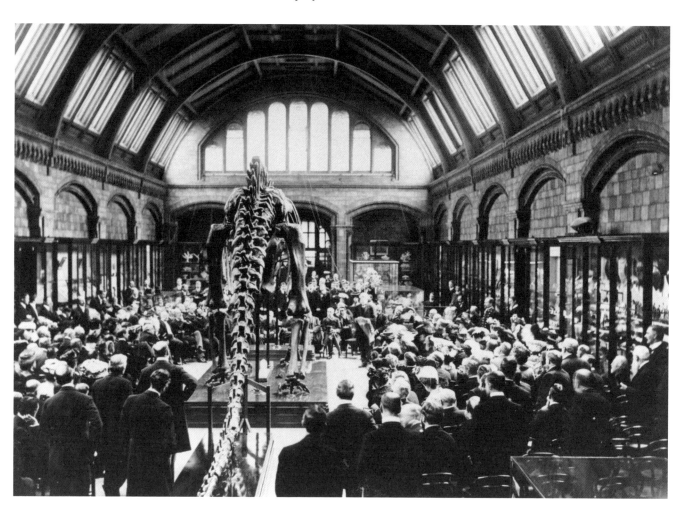

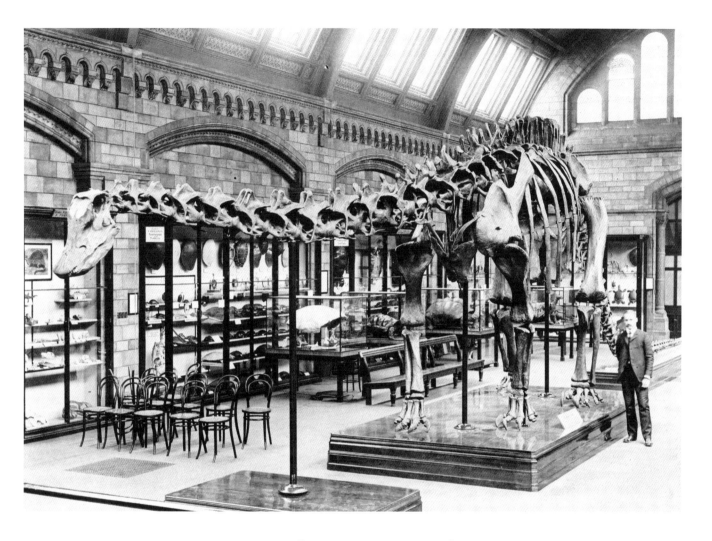

DIPLODOCUS ON DISPLAY, MAY 1904

Thirty-six crates containing the cast of *Diplodocus* arrived in London in February 1904. The Director of the Carnegie Museum, William Holland, came over to oversee the installation, along with Arthur Coggeshall, pictured here, Chief Preparator in the Carnegie's Paleontology Section. This photograph was taken just after the official presentation – the chairs have not been fully cleared away – as *Diplodocus* was first displayed in the Reptile Gallery in the west wing (now part of the Hall of Human Biology).

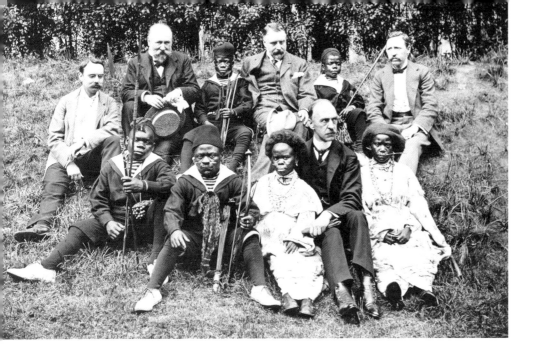

AFRICAN VISITORS, JULY 1905

Six Akka people from the Congo accompanied Colonel James Jonathan Harrison (front row), traveller and photographer, to London in 1905, appearing at the London Hippodrome before touring the country. They went back with Harrison to his home, Brandesburton Hall in the East Riding of Yorkshire, but returned after two years to the Ituri Forest. Whilst in London they visited the Museum, where they found many of the animals in the Mammal Galleries were familiar to them from their homeland.

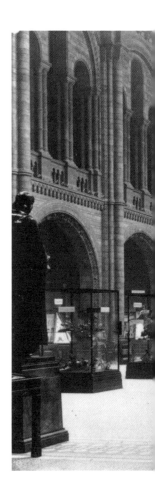

DISPLAY CASES IN CENTRAL HALL, APRIL 1906

This grand vista of the Central Hall sweeps from the bronze statue of Sir Richard Owen by Thomas Brock to the marble statue of Charles Darwin on the staircase. For the next twenty years, Darwin stared down on his former opponent, who disagreed with his theory of evolution. On entry, the visitor encountered display cases illustrating natural history principles and points of interest, a contrast to most gallery layouts where strict scientific classification ruled. The five bays or alcoves on each side of the Hall, known collectively as the Index Museum, housed spectacular specimens and displays providing explanations on the structure of animal and plant life and descriptive terminology.

Young chimpanzee skeleton, July 1907

This little chimpanzee, brought to England from Angola by a sailor, died in April 1698, soon after its arrival. Two months later, Dr Edward Tyson, a leading member of the Royal Society, undertook a groundbreaking study of the 66 cm (26 in) long animal, which was covered in straight, coal-black hair. The dissection is thought to be one of the earliest in England, and Tyson published his results the following year, although misidentifying the chimpanzee as an orang-utan. He concluded incorrectly that it was the 'pygmy' described by classical writers, and represented the missing link between animals and men. The skeleton was presented to the Museum in 1894.

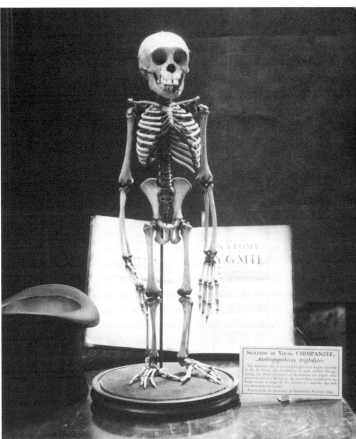

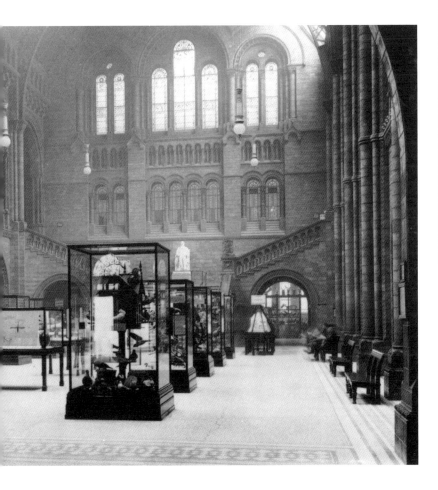

Johnston's okapi, July 1907

In Darkest Africa, Sir Henry Morton Stanley's account of his 1887–89 explorations, included references to a hitherto unknown, ass-like animal. A cross between a giraffe, zebra and antelope, this shy and elusive creature grazed in Ituri forest clearings along the Semliki River, northeastern Zaire. Described as the "crowning zoological discovery of the nineteenth century", Sir Harry Johnston, High Commissioner of Uganda, eventually obtained a skin of what local people called an 'okapi'. In August 1901 this sensational creature was put on display at the Museum. Six years later Sir Benjamin Stone photographed it in the Museum Board Room.

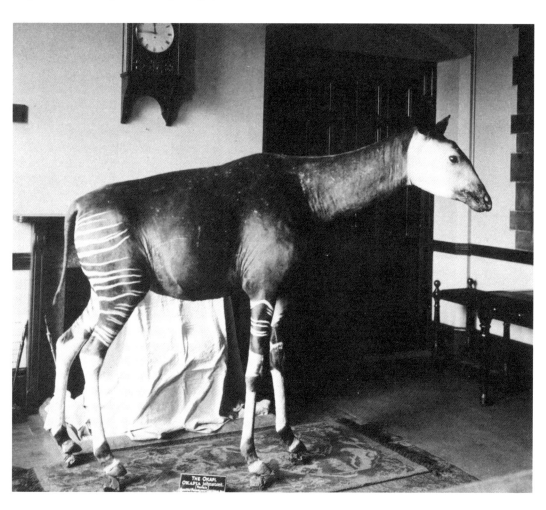

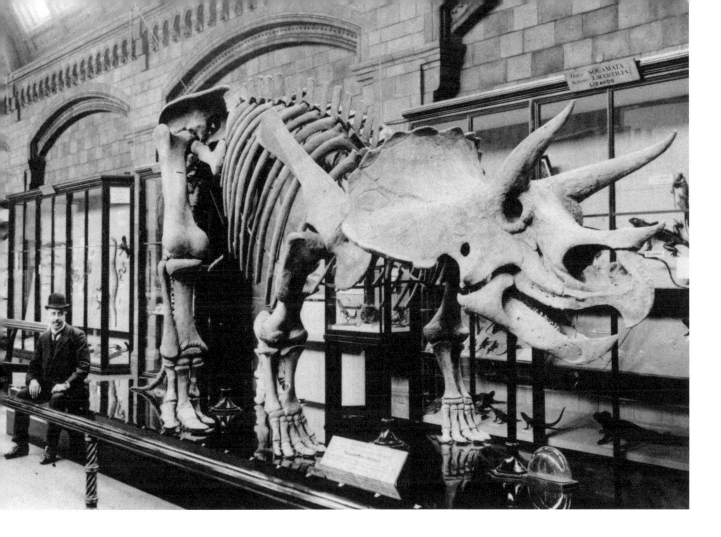

TRICERATOPS PRORSUS, 1907

In 1888 John Bell Hatcher, a protégé of Yale University Professor Othniel Charles Marsh, found the remains of several Mesozoic horned dinosaurs at a ranch in Niobrara County, Wyoming. Marsh, praised by Charles Darwin and Thomas Huxley for finding much supporting evidence for the theory of evolution, named this monster '*Triceratops*' ('three-horned face'). In 1907, the Museum obtained a model from Washington's National Museum of Natural History, for display alongside the *Diplodocus* and *Iguanodon* in the Reptile Gallery. No doubt it was a highlight of a visit that April by Queen Alexandra, the Empress Marie-Féodorovna of Russia and HRH Princess Victoria.

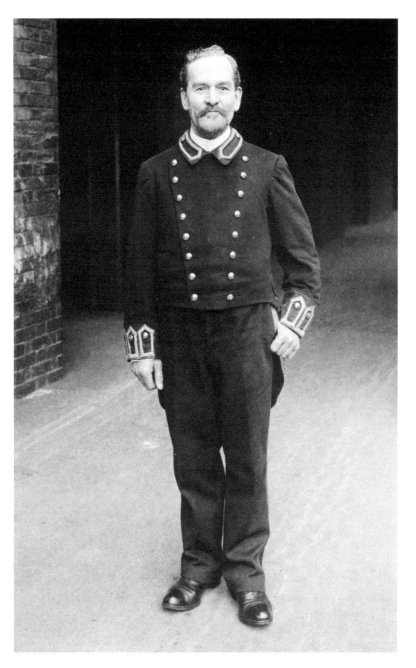

ASHTON J. JONES, CHIEF MESSENGER, 1907

Born in Harefield, Middlesex, Ashton John Jones was the Museum's Chief Messenger for 28 years until his retirement in March 1908. He applied for the post while working at the British Museum as a 2nd Class Assistant in the Department of Printed Books, which he had joined aged 28 in March 1871. The move represented a significant promotion. In addition to this fine uniform and an official apartment at South Kensington, he also received a special annual allowance for superintending the sale of guidebooks from May 1881.

THE GENERAL LIBRARY, 1909

The Librarian, Bernard Barham Woodward (seated right), transferred from the Printed Books Department at the British Museum in 1881 to run the new General Library at South Kensington. Shown here in 1909 with cataloguer Miss A.E. Wilson and Attendant Charles Hadrill, Woodward built up the Library with help from the antiquarian bookseller Frederick Justen of Dulau & Co. Nicknamed 'Bumble Bee' due to his bristly nature, his brother Horace Bolingbroke Woodward, a geologist, was known as 'Humble Bee'. They were nephews to Henry Woodward pictured on p. 12.

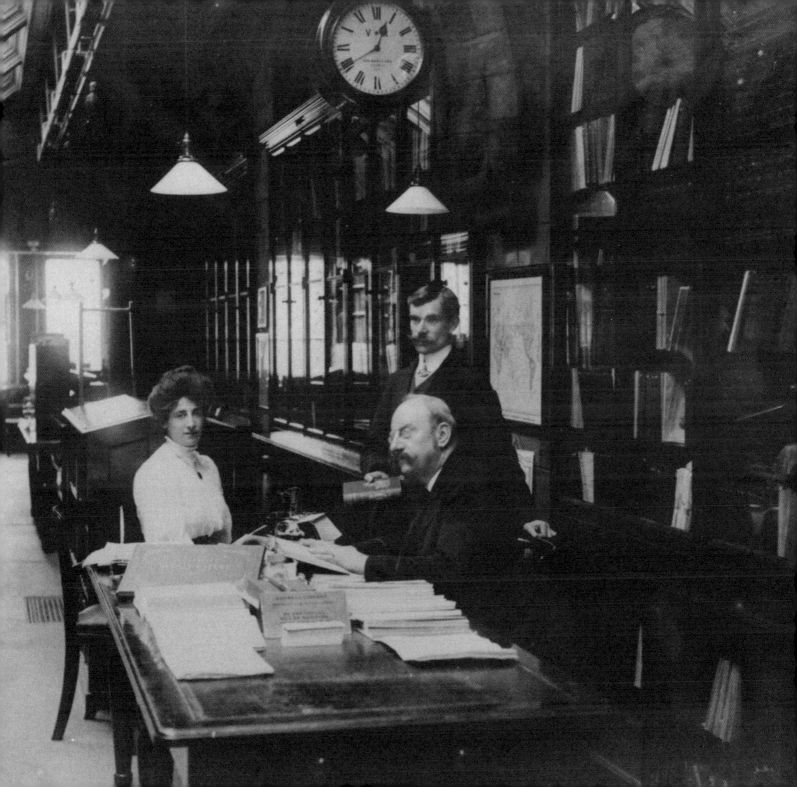

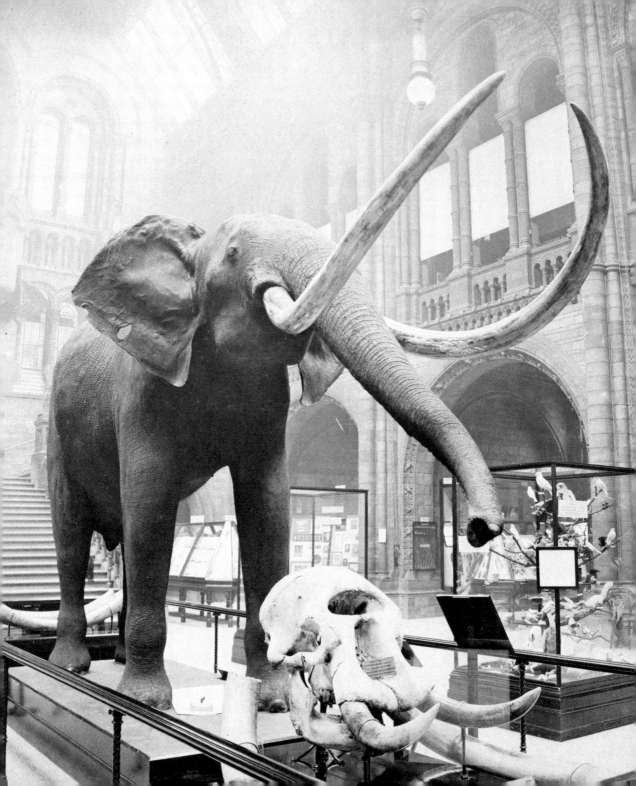

African elephant in Central Hall, February 1910

Photographed in 1910 just three years after his arrival, the African elephant later nicknamed 'George' by journalists, was obtained from the taxidermists Rowland Ward Ltd. The largest pachyderm on public display at 3.5 m (11½ ft) high, T.A. Barns shot him near Mchingi, Malawi. After a period of sliding visitor numbers the Director, Edwin Ray Lankester, arranged for his installation in the Central Hall as a new, crowd-pulling attraction. In contrast to his size a pigmy shrew, the smallest terrestrial mammal, was placed between his feet. Visitor figures did improve and a succession of pachyderms was displayed in the Central Hall until the *Diplodocus* cast moved there in 1979.

Firemen, c. 1910

In 1906, telephonic fire alarms were installed that linked ten points around the Museum with the Firemen's Room in the basement and the local Fire Brigade station. From the opening day until 1971, the staff included firemen warders who patrolled the buildings and grounds day and night. The Chief Officer of the London Fire Brigade made regular inspections of the equipment, which were recorded in a logbook; in 1912 there were 2530 m (8300 ft) of fire-hose, besides two handpumps, four hose trucks and a hose cart. The firemen's uniform around the time of this photograph was a blue cloth tunic, serge jumper, nap overcoat and cap.

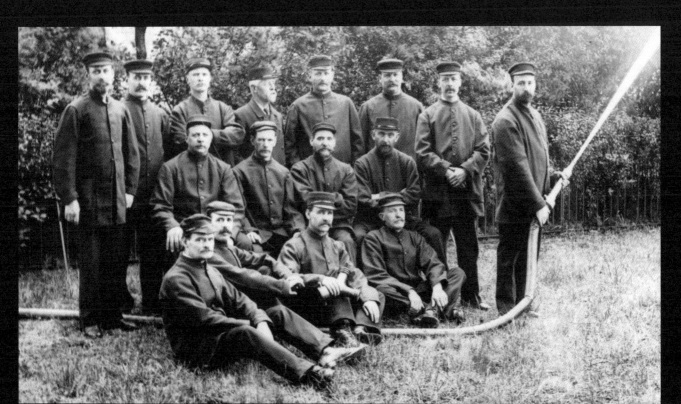

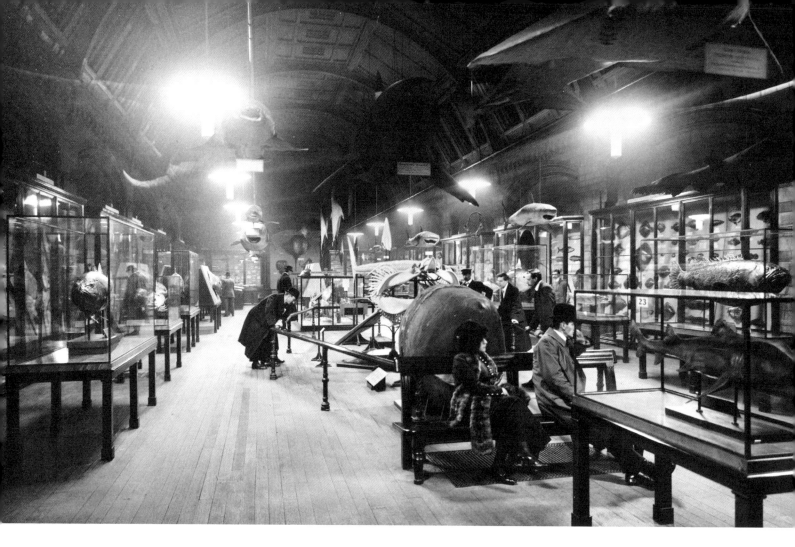

ELECTRIC LIGHTING, MARCH 1911

This picture was taken in March 1911 for a commemorative album compiled by the Union Electric Company Ltd., who were responsible for installing electric lighting in the public galleries. The Trustees had approved the Company's arc lamps for use in the Central and North Halls and the Fish Gallery in February 1908, and the system was gradually extended throughout the Museum over the next decade. The new lighting was popular with visitors, since the Museum could now stay open on dark winter afternoons – although perhaps not so popular with staff who were now required to work later.

SHELL GALLERY, MAY 1911

New attractions for visitors in 1907, four years before this image was taken, included life-size models of an octopus and a giant squid in the Shell Gallery (now the Jerwood Gallery). One observer wrote that the models looked like a "grotesque chandelier and a torpedo". The principal food of sperm whales is squid, including giant squid which can reach a length of 18 m (60 ft) and are widely distributed. These cephalopods are now believed to be the origin for Kraken sea monsters of Norse legend.

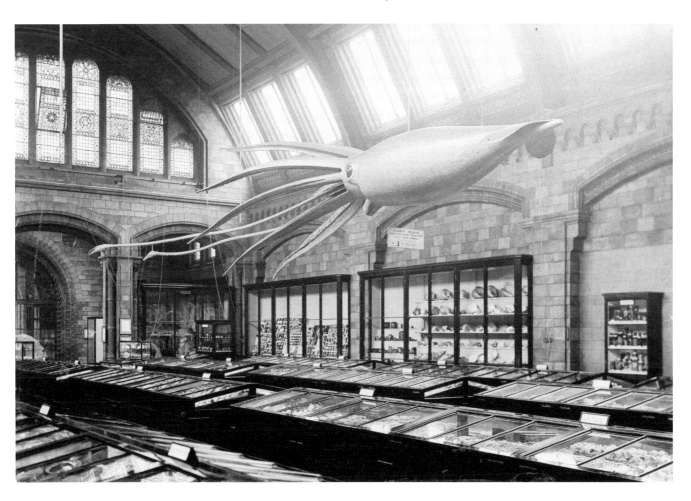

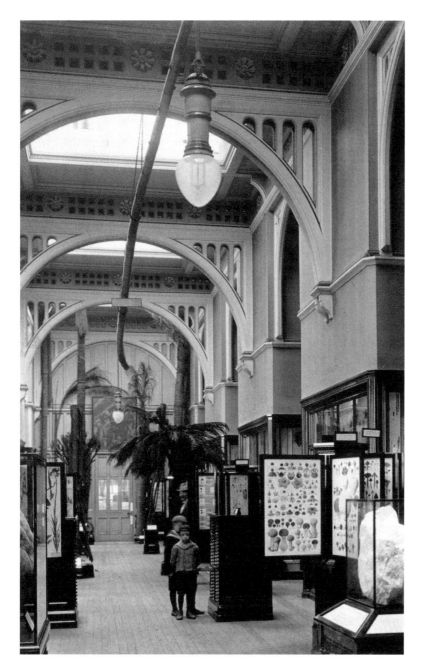

BOTANY EXHIBITION GALLERY, MAY 1911

The light, airy gallery on the top floor of the east wing was dedicated to plants and fungi until 1940, when bombing completely destroyed it (see p.96). Exhibits ranged from large, free-standing palms at the far end to the white bulk of 'diatomaceous earth' near the entrance, composed of the remains of billions of diatoms (a group of microscopic single-celled algae). Suspended from the ceiling was a 24 m (81 ft) 'wabo' bamboo from Burma (Myanmar). British plants were displayed in cabinets and glazed frames fixed to uprights. The boys here are examining the lichens. Below a life-size photograph of an orchid from the Philippines, the door at the end led into the Herbarium, where only staff and scientific students were allowed.

AUGUSTUS H. BISHOP WITH ELEPHANT TUSKS, MAY 1912

Augustus Bishop arrived at the Museum in 1904, aged 23, after three years at taxidermists Messrs. E. Ripley of Richmond. Two years later he was appointed temporary Taxidermist, a post he retained for the next thirteen years until being taken onto the permanent staff. Despite posing with elephant tusks here, Bishop spent much of his career working on bird specimens. In 1911 he was sent bird-collecting in Ireland, and two years after that joined the ornithologist David Bannerman's expedition to the Canary Islands. Relocated to Tring at the outbreak of World War II, Bishop remained there for the rest of his life, continuing to work part-time after his retirement.

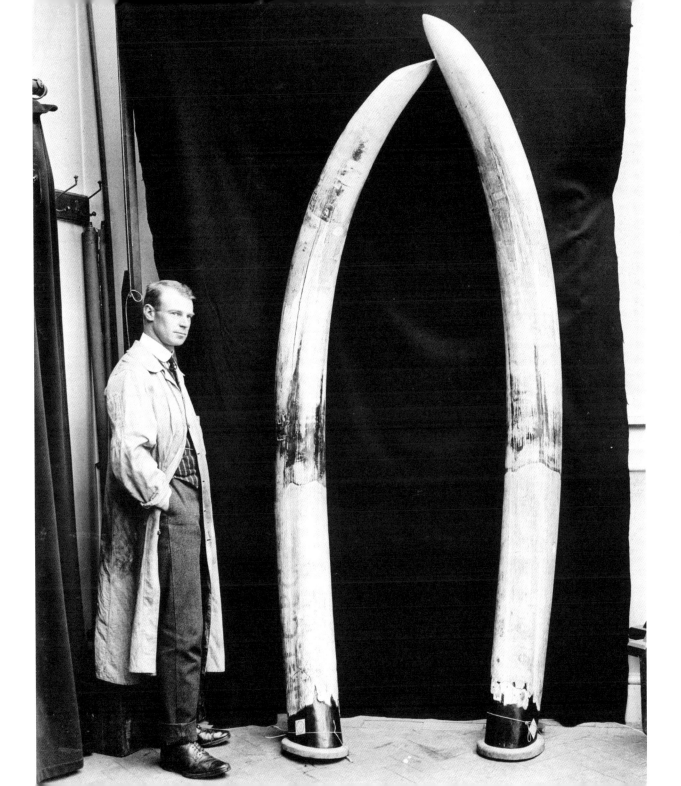

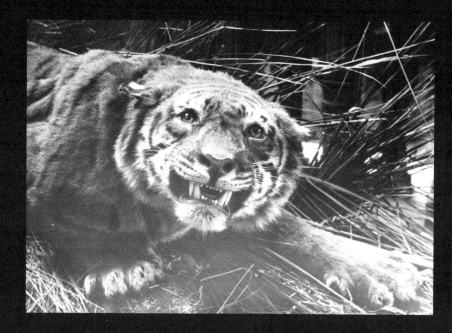

Bengal tiger, 1913

The tradition of royal gifts and loans to the Museum dates back to the early years of the British Museum, when in 1757 George II presented the Royal Library, comprising some 12,000 volumes, to the nation. George V continued this royal practice, in 1913 offering this tiger and the head of an Indian rhinoceros that he shot in Nepal. The tiger skin was mounted and, along with the rhinoceros head, put on display at the top of the stairs on the second floor, near the Hume Collection of Heads and Horns of Big Game which adorned the walls.

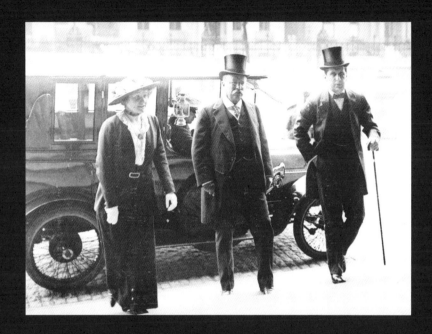

Roosevelt visiting, June 1914

Ex-President Theodore Roosevelt spent the morning of 16 June 1914 sightseeing in London, one of his destinations being the Natural History Museum. Here, he is seen with Museum Trustee Viscount Dillon and his wife. According to *The Times*, Roosevelt was particularly interested in the antelopes, the new gorilla from near Lake Tanganyika, the Selous collection of big game, and the illustrations of protective colouration. Frederick Courtenay Selous, a famous 19th century big game hunter, had organised and accompanied Roosevelt's hunting expedition in British East Africa (roughly Kenya and Uganda) in 1909–10.

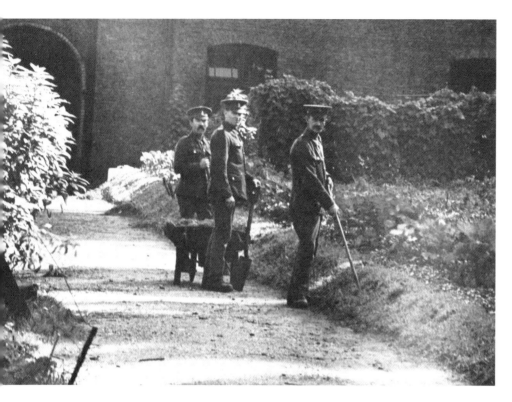

SOLDIERS IN GROUNDS, 1917

During World War I a 'war farm' was established at the eastern end of the grounds, tended by staff and convalescent soldiers. Potatoes, cauliflowers, artichokes and 'green crops' were grown for distribution amongst troops stationed in the area, and chickens, rabbits, and eight pedigree black Sussex pigs "developed amazingly". The fate of the chickens and rabbits is unknown, but the pigs "ultimately made a profit of between £60 and £70 and provided excellent Christmas dinners for the men for whom the usual Christmas fare was not procurable".

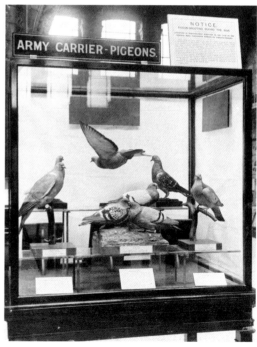

PIGEON TYPES, C. 1918

As food shortages hit during World War I, carrier pigeons that saved lives by relaying messages from downed pilots or disabled ships sometimes ended up shot for pigeon pie. Just one bird released by Thomas Crisp VC, the mortally wounded skipper of a damaged auxiliary patrol fishing boat, ensured the rescue of his entire crew. To highlight the vital differences between wood pigeons, rock doves and stock doves and their carrier cousins, the Museum obtained several racing pigeons for this display in 1916 from the famous breeder, Colonel A.H. Osman. His birds won many races and their descendants are still prized today by pigeon fanciers.

INDIAN SOLDIERS AT ENTRANCE, 15 AUGUST 1919

Over 130,000 Indian soldiers served in World War I. Casualties from the Western Front were hospitalised in Britain, and the Brighton Royal Pavilion was converted into the Indian Hospital, complete with multiple kitchens for different faiths. Having taken part in the Victory Parade on Peace Day, 19 July 1919, soon after the signing of the Versailles Treaty, the Indian Contingent was given the opportunity to visit the Museum. Over several days in August, an official guide was put at the disposal of the parties of officers and men, who had probably joined other Allied troops bivouacking in Kensington Gardens during the celebrations.

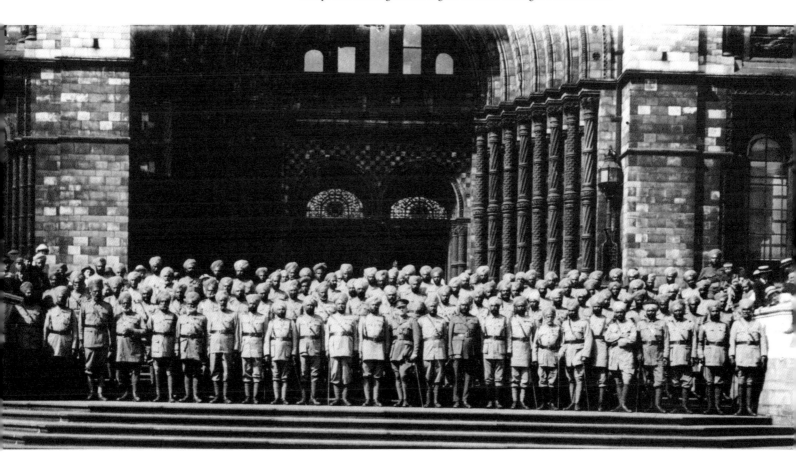

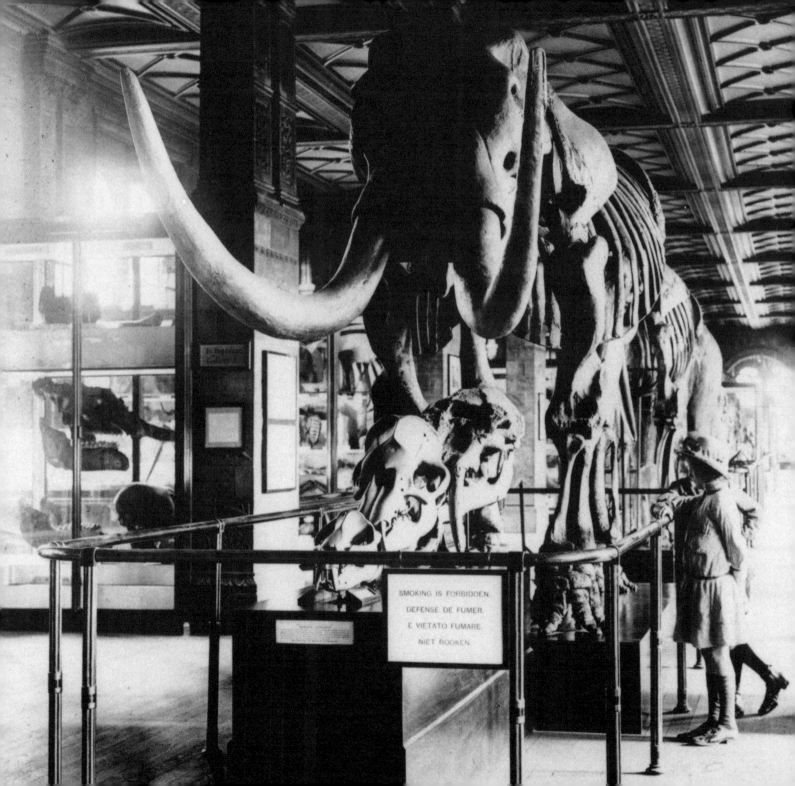

SMOKING IS FORBIDDEN.

DEFENSE DE FUMER.

E VIETATO FUMARE.

NIET ROOKEN.

MASTODON IN GEOLOGICAL GALLERY, DECEMBER 1919

The Guide Lecturer, John Henry Leonard, took this shot of two girls inspecting a primitive elephant or Mastodon (*Mammut americanum*), in December 1919. Found in Benton County, Missouri, it greeted visitors at the entrance to the east wing of the ground floor fossil mammal displays. This partially reconstructed skeleton has an unusual history – Professor Richard Owen purchased it in 1844 after seeing it described as a 'Missouri Leviathan', exhibited with other American fossils by the showman Albert Koch at the Egyptian Hall, Piccadilly. Owen disentangled the Mastodon from the many bones which had been added, proving it was not a new, distinct species.

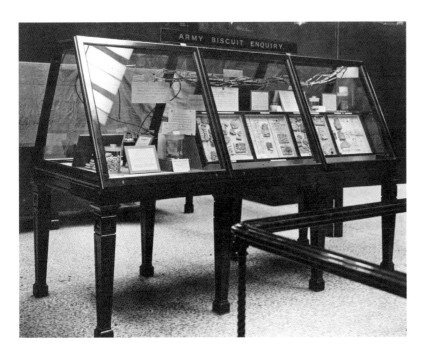

ARMY BISCUIT ENQUIRY, 1920s

This display was the result of a request for help from the War Office in 1910. Troops in South Africa and Mauritius had discovered that biscuits sent out in supposedly hermetically sealed tins had been infested with moths, and become inedible. John Hartley Durrant of the Zoology Department was given the task of investigating this phenomenon, concluding that the eggs must have been laid between baking and packing the biscuits, and larvae had developed later inside the sealed tins.

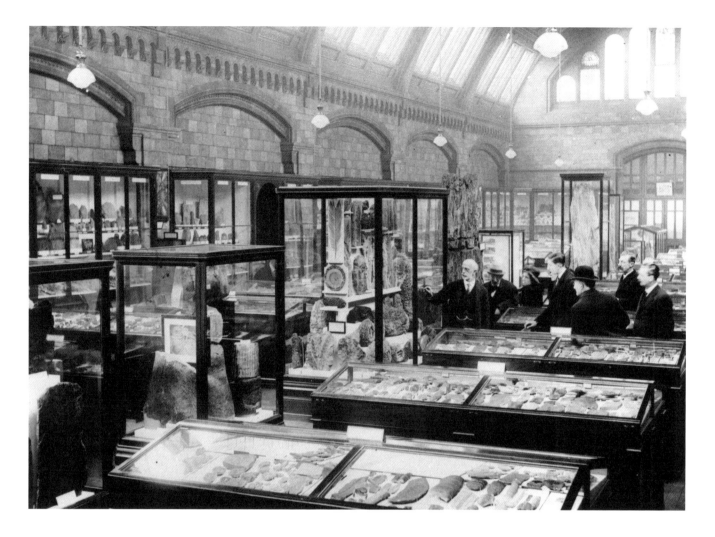

JOHN H. LEONARD, GUIDE LECTURER, WITH VISITORS, C. 1920

Following Lord Sudeley's campaign to make museums more attractive and interesting, former teacher John Henry Leonard was appointed as the first Guide Lecturer on a trial basis in May 1912. After six months, the public had been so appreciative and Leonard had proved himself so "capable and zealous in the discharge of his duties" – comprising twice-daily tours of the exhibits – that his services were retained until his death in 1931.

GIRL WITH DINOSAUR BONE, 1920s

In the Fossil Reptile gallery, this young woman holds a yardstick against a cast of the right humerus or upper arm bone of *Tornieria africana*, named in 1911 after German palaeontologist, Gustav Tornier. Excavations of the largest dinosaur fossils began in 1909 at Tendagaru, Tanganyika and the amazing finds were sent to Stuttgart and Berlin museums. Soon after this photograph was taken, funds were raised for a British Museum East African Expedition, from 1924 until 1931, led by William Cutler and then Frederick Migeod with assistance from the famous anthropologist Louis Leakey. From this single bone measuring 2 m (7 ft 1 in), scientists calculated *Tornieria* stood 6 m (20 ft) high at the shoulder.

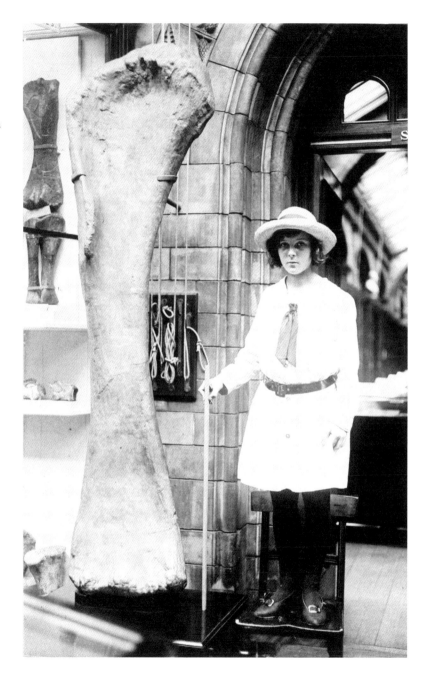

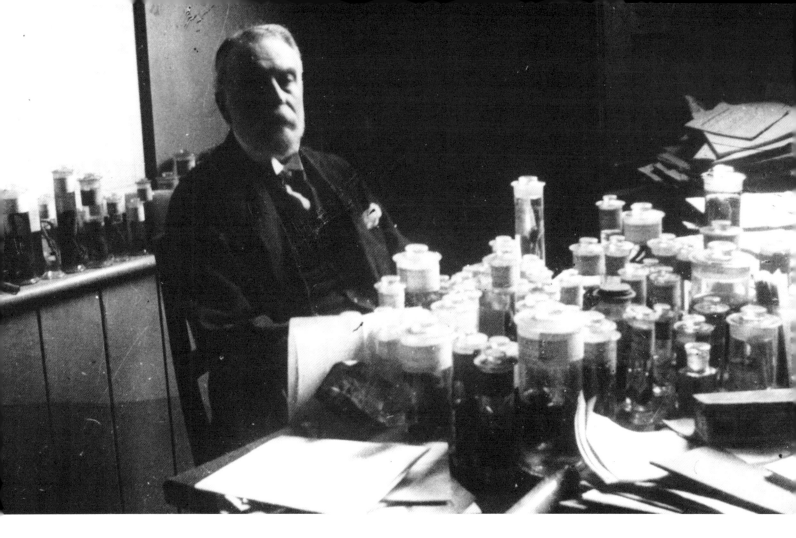

Georges A. Boulenger with spirit jars, 1920s

Belgian Georges Boulenger (1858–1937) started cataloguing the reptile collections after meeting the Keeper of Zoology in the public galleries in 1881. Boulenger had previously worked at the Musée Royal d'Histoire Naturelle in Brussels, and was given responsibility for the spirit collections – glass jars of specimens preserved in alcohol. In 1882 he was appointed 1st Class Assistant, and over the next 38 years became world famous for his work on reptiles and fish. With an excellent memory and language skills, he was a very hard worker – besides having a noted ability to fall asleep anytime, anywhere. On retirement he returned to Belgium and applied his expertise to the study of roses.

Unveiling Selous memorial, June 1920

Frederick Courtenay Selous (1851–1917) was one of the most famous big game hunters of his era. He spent much of his life in Africa, but also hunted in North America and Asia Minor. Many of his specimens were sent here to South Kensington, and when he was killed in action at Beho Beho in modern-day Tanzania, it was decided that the Museum would be the most appropriate place for a memorial. The bronze bust by William Colton (to the left of the elephant head), set in granite from the Zimbabwean Matoppo Hills, was unveiled in the Central Hall on 10 June 1920, before a guard of honour of Boy Scouts.

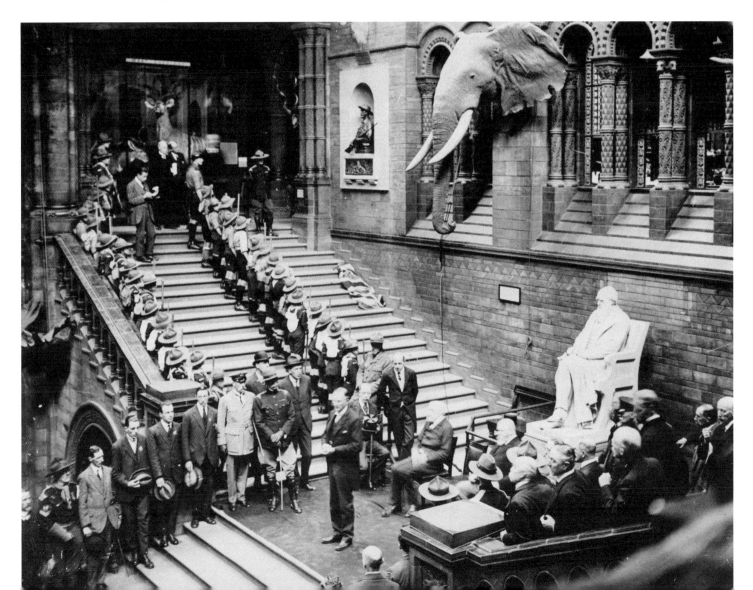

CHARLES BADCOCK, GATEKEEPER, C. 1920

Charles Badcock, Police Constable no. 209, began work at the Museum in 1902, aged 43. In 1910 he joined the Museum staff as a front gatekeeper, and was provided with the uniform that he is wearing here – a blue cloth tunic and trousers, and a hat with a 2 cm (³/4 in) wide gold band. The medal on the right is the Khedive of Egypt's Bronze Star, awarded to British soldiers who served in the Egyptian Campaign in the 1880s. Discipline at the Museum was strict – in 1903 one gatekeeper forfeited two days' leave for allowing unauthorised persons into the front-gate lodge. Badcock died in service on 13 March 1926.

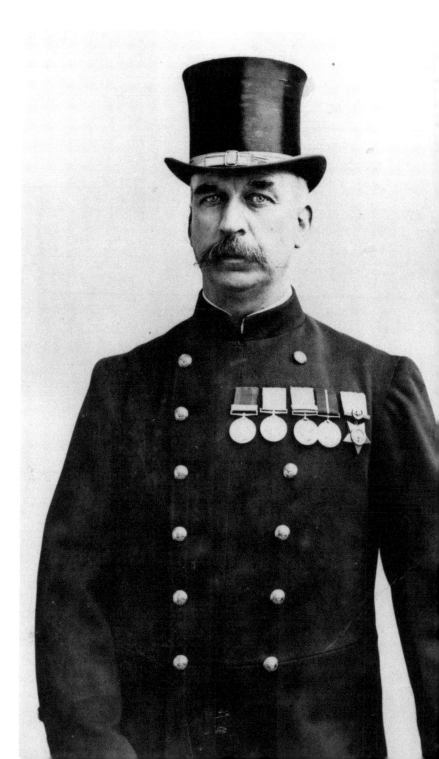

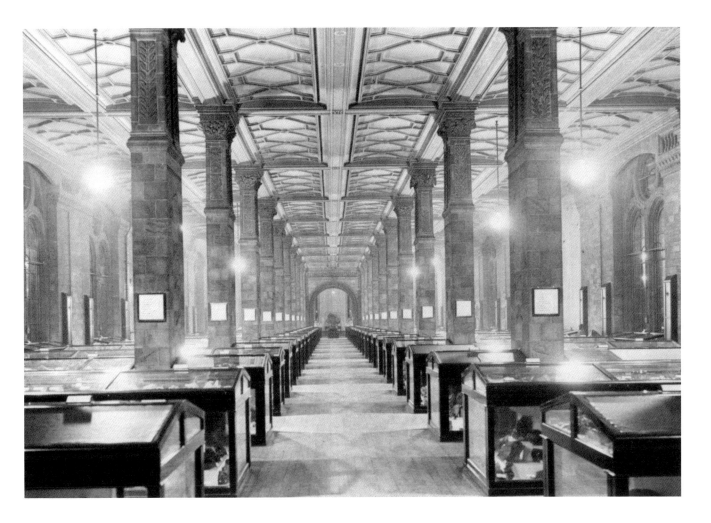

MINERAL GALLERY, 1923

The Mineral Gallery, on the first floor of the east wing, is the only area to retain the same layout since first opening in 1881. Rocks, minerals and meteorites were arranged according to chemical composition and crystalline form. At the time of this picture in 1923, the pavilion at the eastern end of the gallery was dedicated to larger mineral specimens including the 3.5 tonne Cranbourne meteorite, which can be seen in the centre at the far end. Found in 1854 in Victoria, Australia, it was relocated elsewhere in the Museum when the pavilion was redeveloped as The Vault in 2007.

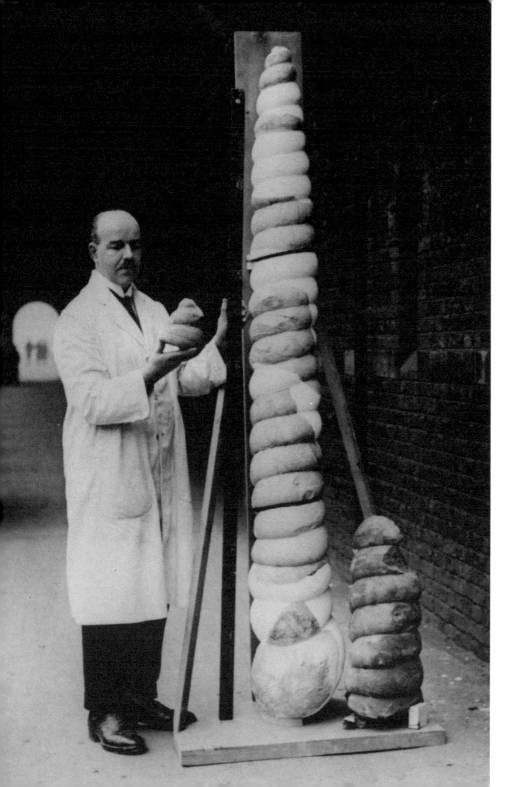

A Wealden mollusc, 1924

One of the preparators in the Geology Department, Frank Oswell Barlow, seen here with his reconstruction of a giant Wealden mollusc, arrived at the Museum in 1896 to serve an unpaid three-year apprenticeship with his father, Caleb. Responsible for fine casts of the fossil bird, *Archaeopteryx*, and Piltdown Man, Frank retired in 1941. Between them father and son had contributed 79 years' service. Described as having "a massively imposing figure and personality", Frank sang at coronations in Westminster Abbey, and his cultured conversation and courteous approach led to him being mistaken for the Museum Director or a Trustee on more than one occasion.

Preparing models, c. 1924

Percy and Stuart Stammwitz, seen here adding details to a replica horse, were responsible for preparing models and mounted specimens required for gallery displays by the Zoology Department. Model-making techniques were often handed down from father to son – for example, the Geology Department employed Caleb and Frank Oswell Barlow, and Louis Emmanuel and Robert John Parsons. The younger generation often developed innovative methods of displaying specimens using the latest materials such as plastics.

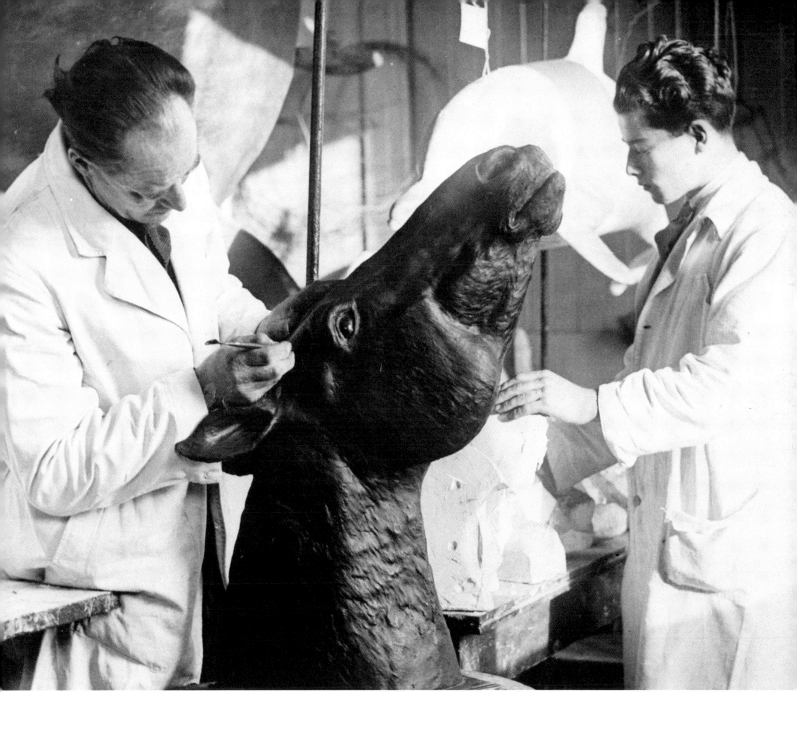

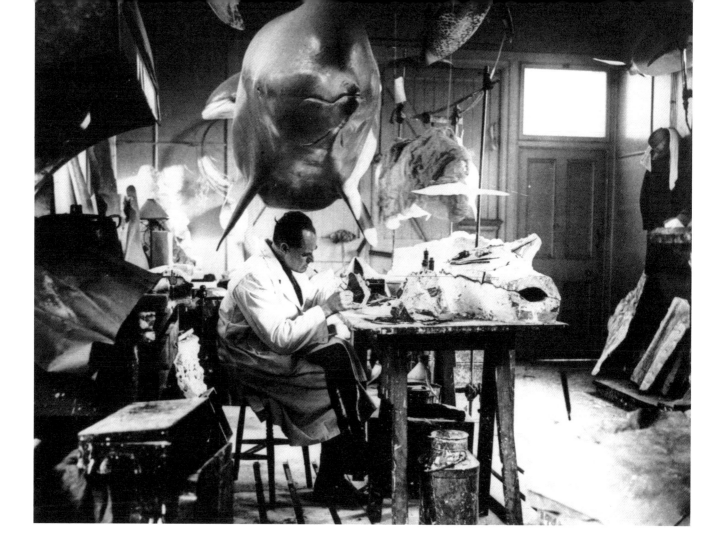

DOLPHIN CASTING, C. 1924

Percy Stammwitz, the skilled technician captured here in the Preparators'
Workshop making casts of dolphins for models in the proposed new Whale Hall,
joined the Museum in 1906. While carrying out this laborious process, he may
have recalled his exciting trip during 1913–14 as an eager young assistant on Major
Gerald Barrett-Hamilton's expedition to South Georgia, near the Falkland Islands.
The harsh weather conditions, described in Barrett-Hamilton's notebook, probably
seemed a lifetime ago to Percy, hard at work in South Kensington a decade later.

Dugong casting, c. 1924

To avoid the results of deterioration, it was vital to prepare casts from the bodies of large cetaceans and other mammals, such as this rare dugong, as soon as they arrived at the Museum. No doubt Percy Stammwitz found working on this unusual creature, often described as a mermaid by early mariners, an interesting challenge. In 1925, a newspaper article revealed a glimpse of Percy's own artistic flair and personality. His new home at Sunbury-on-Thames was constructed along the lines of a Middle Eastern mosque complete with minarets.

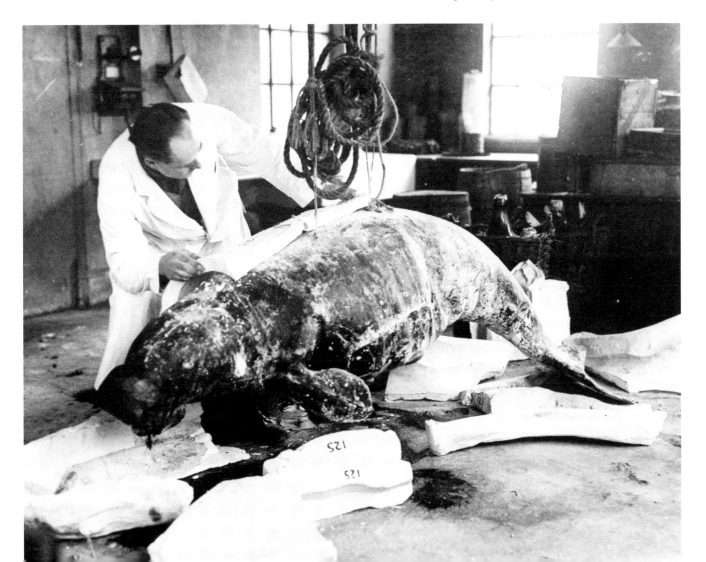

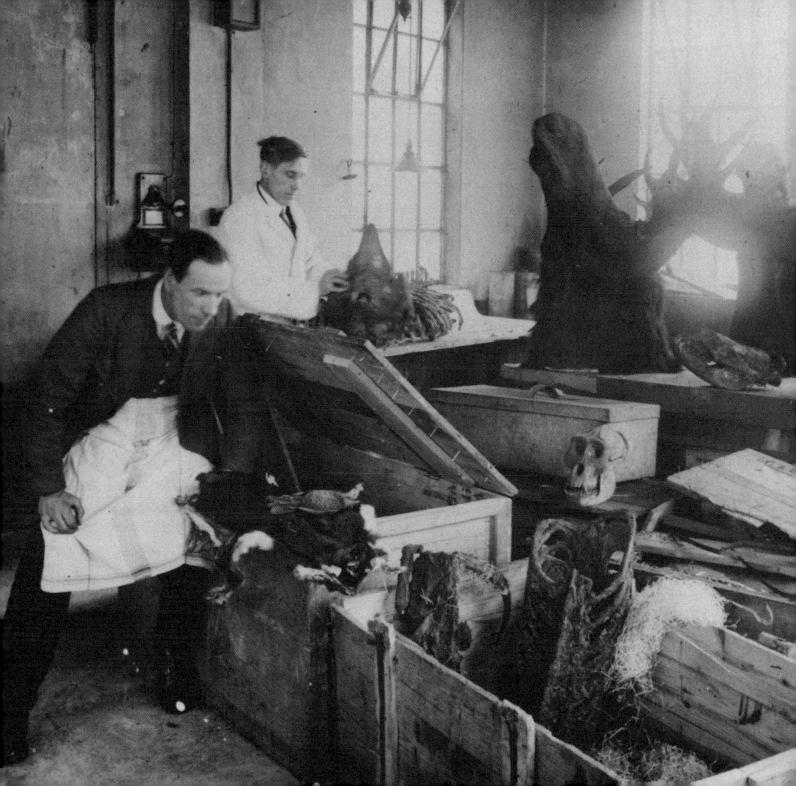

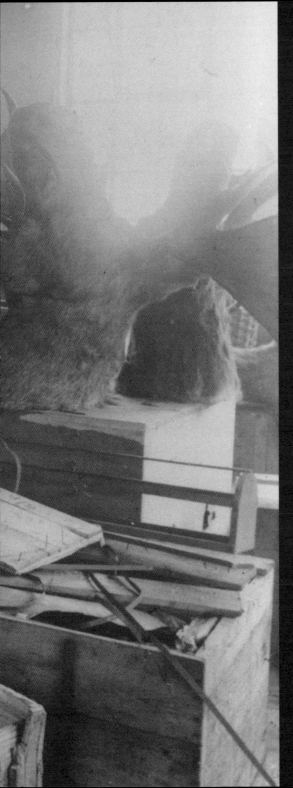

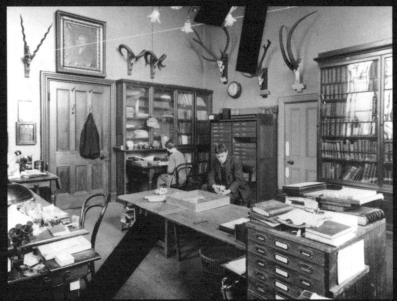

ZOOLOGY UNPACKING ROOM, 1924

Following a four-year delay due to boundary discussions with the proposed new Science Museum, an Unpacking Room for zoological specimens opened for business in early 1912 at the rear of the Museum. Here attendants unpacked the many wooden crates of specimens that arrived each year from all corners of the globe. Addressed 'London, Museum', these cases contained animal skins and dislocated skeletons nestling in wood shavings for protection against damage in transit. While four moose heads gaze at the ceiling in the background, a wall-mounted telephone enabled staff to inform departments when long-awaited deliveries arrived.

MAMMAL STUDY, 1924

Copied from a glass lantern slide, its cracks crudely repaired with black tape, this image features Martin Alister Campbell Hinton, soon after his appointment as an assistant in the Zoology Department, with temporary worker Nancy Kaye. Volunteering in the Palaeontology Department from 1905 and something of a prodigy as well as a noted practical joker, Martin later became Keeper of Zoology, retiring in 1945. Various ungulate horns, some from the Hume Collection, and a portrait of the naturalist Thomas Hardwicke, adorn the walls.

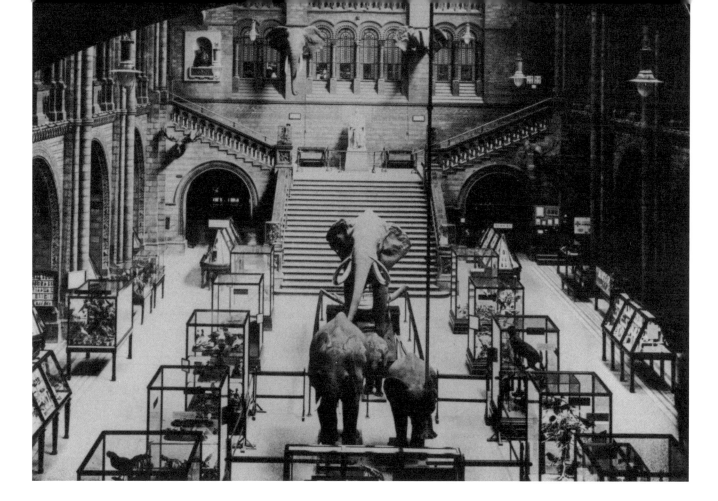

CENTRAL HALL WITH ELEPHANTS AND CASES, C. 1924

This photograph captures the Central Hall at its fullest. Four elephants dominate
the scene: 'George', the largest, is now accompanied by three smaller specimens
from South Africa. John Gould's collection of hummingbirds, purchased for the
Museum in 1881 after his death, sit rather precariously on the staircase columns.
The Refreshment Room, glimpsed through the stained glass windows designed by
Waterhouse and made by F.T. Odell of Finsbury, had been furnished with marble-
topped tables, copper urns and a meat safe by the 1890s, replacing the teak and
mahogany refreshment bars on the second floor.

Scaffolding in Central Hall, 1925

This photograph, taken in February 1925, marked the cleaning and redecoration of the North and Central Halls by the Office of Works. Open to the public since 1881, the grime of an increasingly industrialised London had taken its toll on architect Alfred Waterhouse's terracotta masterpiece. Starting in September 1924, scaffolding was erected and all surfaces carefully washed, and mouldings painted as required. Work finished by July 1925 and the Director recommended to the Trustees that the two halls should receive regular attention in future. Fortunately, damage to surfaces declined following the Smoke Abatement Act passed the following year and the Clean Air Acts of the 1950s and 1960s.

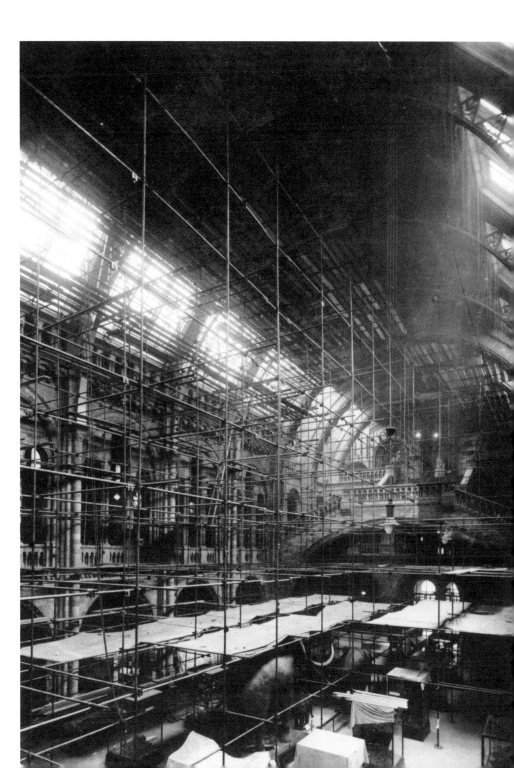

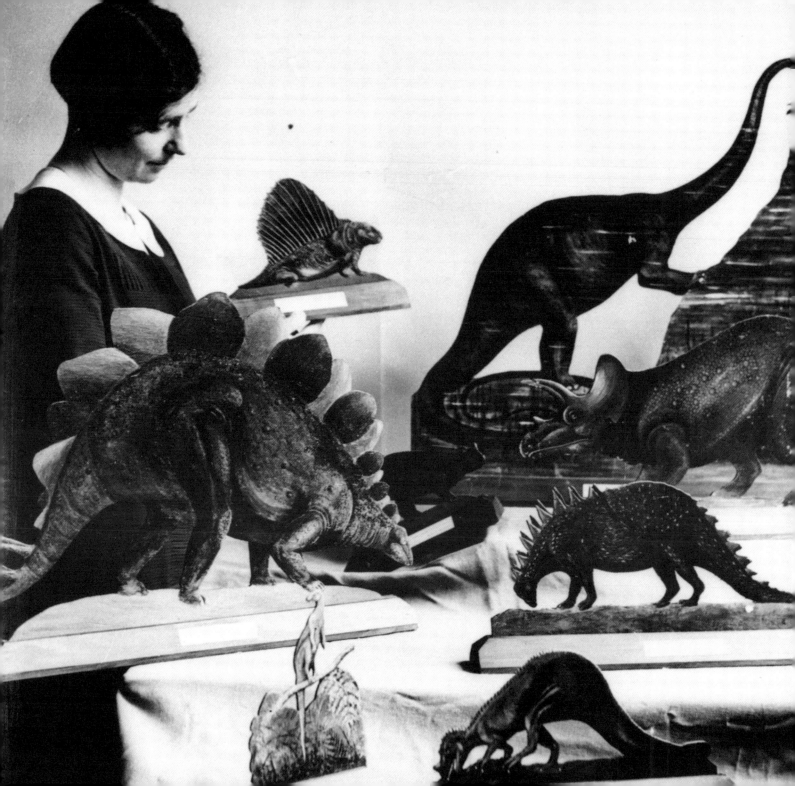

UPNOR ELEPHANT, 1926

In 1911 a party of Royal Engineers cut a practice trench on Tower Hill, Upnor, Kent and disturbed several large bones. Two years later the Museum was alerted, but by the time it came to excavate the bones in 1915 they were severely damaged. Louis Parsons, supervised by Dr Charles Andrews of the Geology Department, carefully extracted the remains of the 100,000-year-old monster, now known as the Upnor elephant, and reconstructed the headless skeleton for display in 1926 around an iron support structure costing some £250.

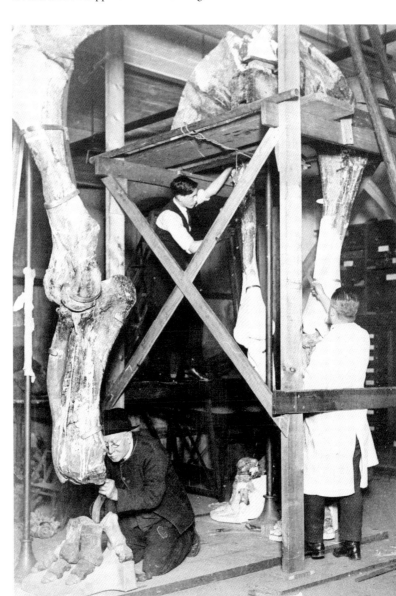

WOMAN WITH DINOSAUR MODELS, 1926

By the mid-1920s when this photograph was taken, children visiting the Museum wanted to take home souvenir models of the dinosaurs on display. Miss Hilda Bather, daughter of Francis Arthur Bather, Keeper of Geology, offered this set of seven dinosaur models for sale from her premises. The models, drawn and painted by artist Vernon Edwards, a former Royal Navy commander, could be purchased for between 6s 6d and £1 10s each. Edwards also made several three-dimensional scale models, used by many museums for educational purposes, and designed a series of fossil fish dioramas on display in the Museum from the late 1930s.

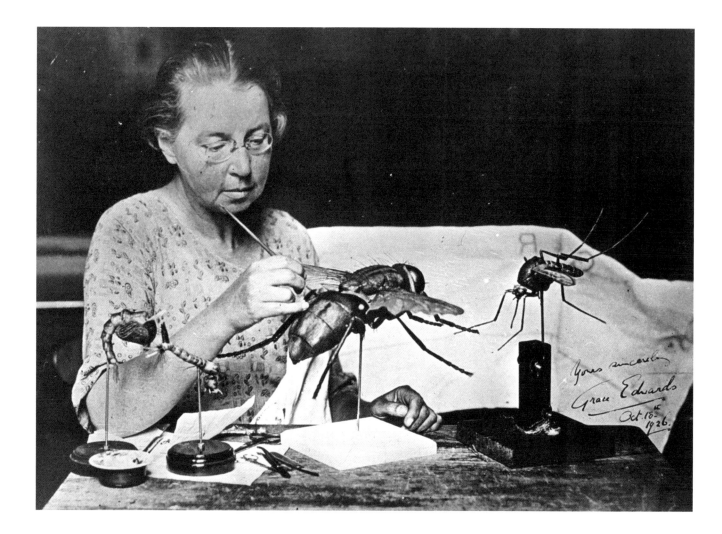

GRACE EDWARDS, OCTOBER 1926

Grace Edwards was employed on an unofficial basis by the Entomology Department to prepare illustrations and models of specimens. She was asked to design a war memorial for the Museum staff who had died during World War I – this can still be seen on the pillar in the Central Hall to the right of the main door as you leave. The models she is working on in this photograph were displayed in cases in the Central Hall for a number of years, and used to teach recruits from the Royal Army Medical Corps about disease-spreading insects.

CROWD AROUND FLEA CASE, 1927

During the first decades of the 20th century, the Central Hall contained a number of exhibit cases explaining the role of insects and other animals in spreading disease. Large models of bloodsuckers such as mosquitoes, tsetses and rat-fleas – the latter shown here in 1927 – were accompanied by displays on houseflies, ticks, lice and the disease bilharziosis, caused by small worms. During World War I the Museum produced a series of popular pamphlets and information posters on the dangers of flies, mosquitoes, bedbugs, lice, ticks and fleas, both for domestic use and for distribution among troops abroad.

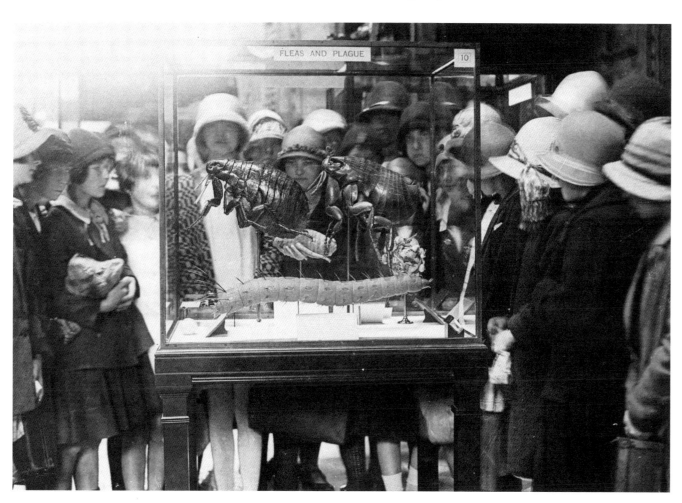

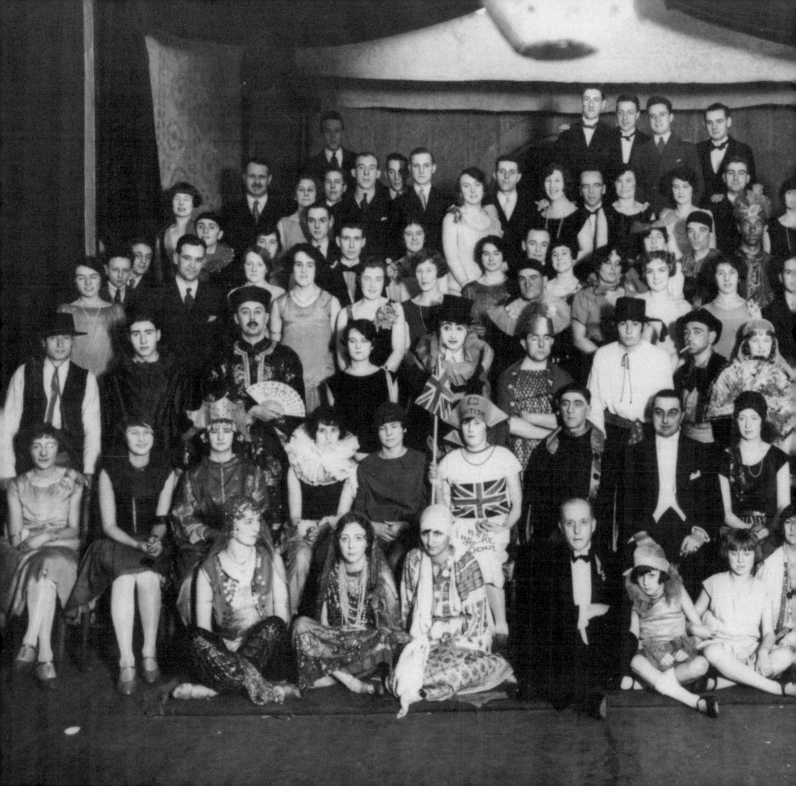

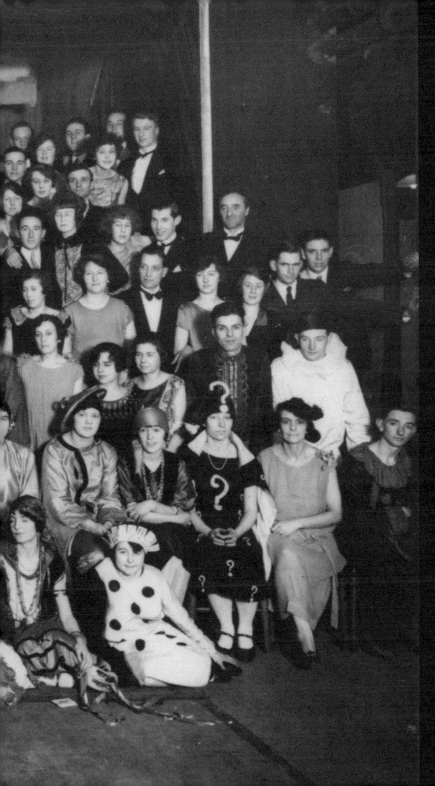

STAFF DANCE, JANUARY 1927

This photo of the staff dance held on New Year's Day 1927 captures the party-going spirit of the Jazz Age. Fancy dress was a popular theme among the post-war generation of 'Bright Young Things', and 'Orientalism' – the West's response to the East – had filtered down to popular music and fashion. Those attending aimed high, costuming themselves as matadors, sheiks and Indians à la Rudolph Valentino in his 1920s films, *Blood and Sand, Son of the Sheik* and *The Young Rajah.* Dancing to recent hit tunes such as *The Piccadilly Strut* and *The Black Bottom Stomp*, captured on new electrical recordings, no doubt it was a memorable occasion.

1920–1929

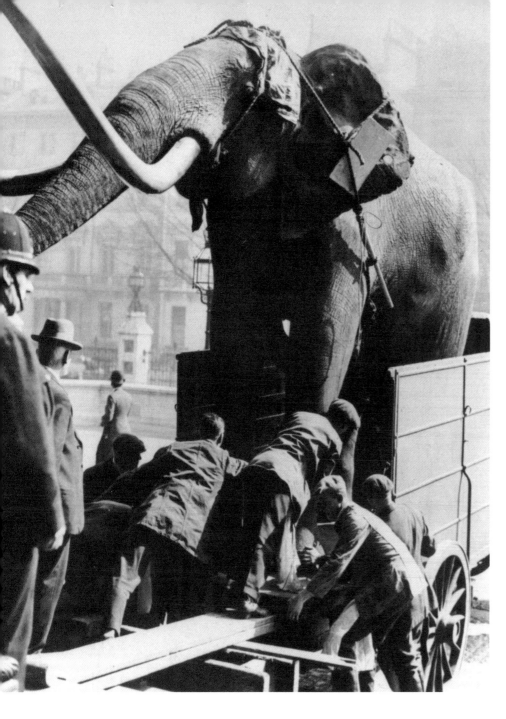

'George' in the entrance, April 1927

The removal of 'George' the African elephant from the Central Hall in April 1927 caused rather a commotion. As the skin had shrunk over time, it was necessary to send him back to the taxidermists, Rowland Ward Ltd., to be remounted. However, as he was manoeuvred, rear first, out of the main door, his large ears proved impossible to fit through the opening. George was left in this rather ignominious position while it was debated over lunch what could be done. Eventually a rope was used to hold the ears back against his head, and George was finally loaded on the cart waiting outside.

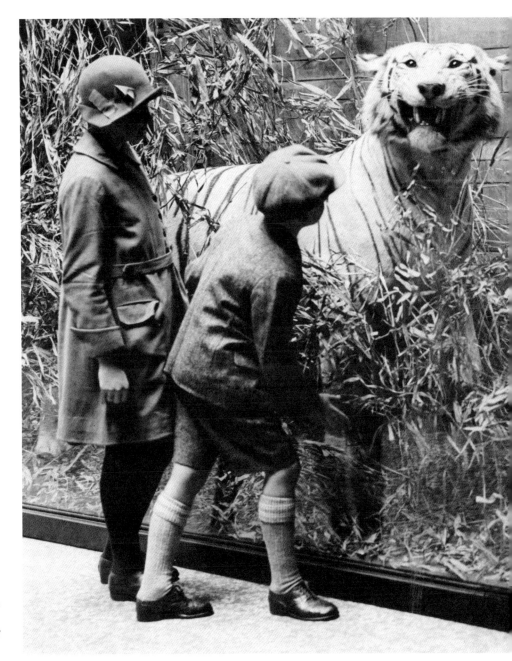

CHILDREN EXAMINING TIGER, C. 1927

This white tiger was shot in the Rewa jungle in early
1925 by the Maharajah Gulab Singh. The Maharajah
was known for organising elaborate hunting parties
for his guests in Rewa, a former princely state in
central India in an area famous for its white tigers.
He presented this animal to George V, who in turn
loaned the specimen to the Museum in February
1926. It was mounted at the Rowland Ward studios in
Piccadilly, and when the King visited in March he
would have seen it displayed opposite the Bengal tiger
(see p. 46) he had presented thirteen years previously.

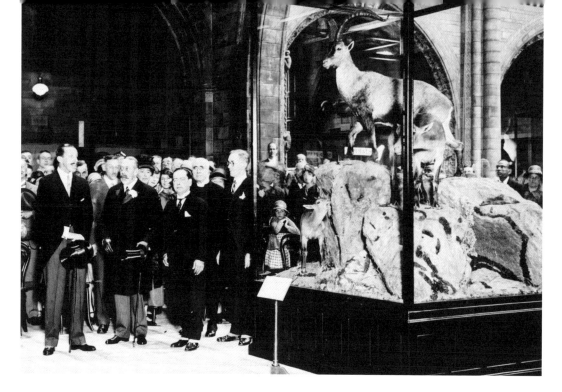

KING OF SPAIN PRESENTING IBEX, 7 JULY 1927

At the request of George V, the presentation of a group
of ibex by King Alfonso of Spain in July 1927 was kept
informal. An unveiling ceremony took place at noon in
the Central Hall, where a Spanish flag had been draped
over the large case containing three specimens of *Capra
pyrenaica Victoriae*, named after the Queen of Spain.
The flag was drawn up into a canopy by means of a
pulley, thus revealing the specimens arranged in their
natural rocky surroundings, which had taken Luis
Benedito of the National Museum of Natural Sciences,
Madrid four months to complete.

DARWIN STATUE, SEPTEMBER 1927

The 2.5 tonne marble statue of Darwin was unveiled in
June 1885 after a worldwide public appeal raised £4500.
Over 2000 subscriptions came from Sweden alone.
The statue by Sir Joseph Boehm cost £2000, and the
remainder of the money went into the Darwin Fund
for the "furtherance of biological science". In 1927 the
Central Hall was rearranged to accommodate an Indian
elephant, and after much heated debate Darwin was
moved nearer the main door via a pulley, rollers and
heavy planks, and the statue of Richard Owen was
installed in his place on the staircase.

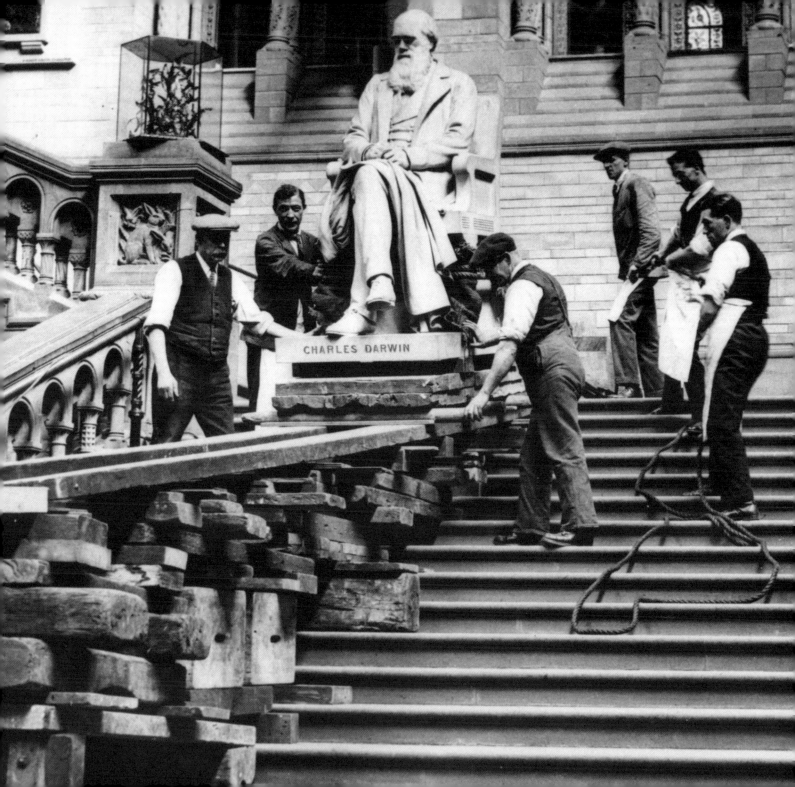

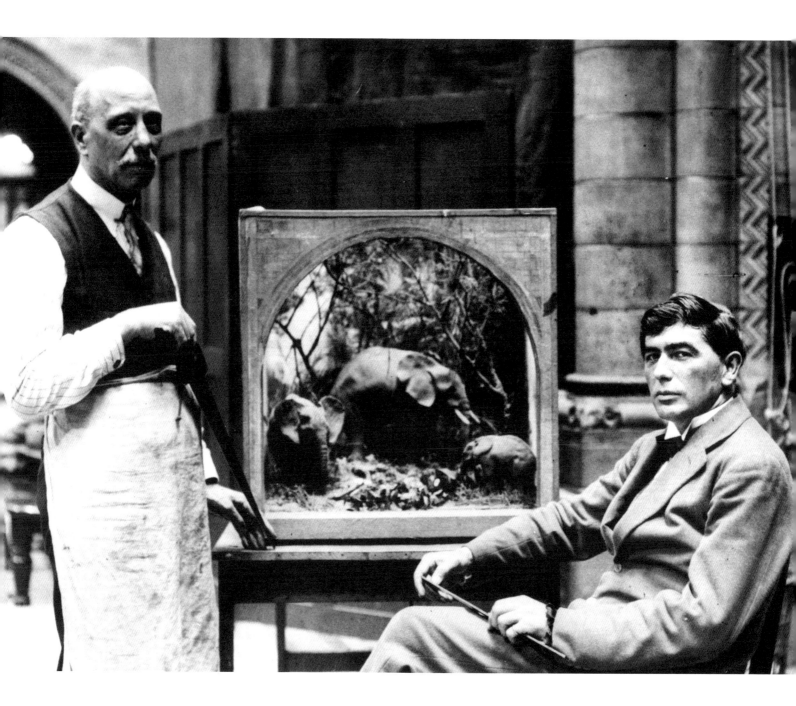

GUY DOLLMAN WITH SMALL-SCALE ELEPHANT MODEL, 1927

Captain Guy Dollman (seated), Assistant Keeper of Zoology, designed this model scene for an innovative, full-sized display in one of the bays in the Central Hall which opened in July 1927. In the full-sized display, three elephants, presented by the government of South Africa, were placed in a recreation of their natural surroundings, the Knysna Forest, accompanied by real timber and vegetation specially prepared to prevent decay. Dr George Herbert-Smith, Assistant Museum Secretary, designed the lighting effects – eight variations, from bright daylight to soft moonlight. Newspaper articles noted that Mrs Dollman had assisted Captain Dollman, who had gained his title during the war.

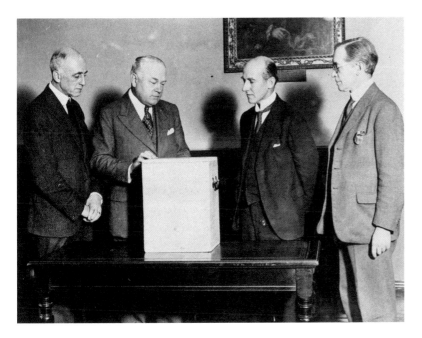

CHANG FILM PRESENTATION, 1927

In 1925 Merian Cooper and Ernest Schoedsack, later co-directors of *King Kong*, devised a 70-minute tale, *Chang*, of a Thai jungle village encountering wild animals, which premiered two years later at the Plaza, Piccadilly Circus. Synchronised recordings of elephants, a bear, a tiger, a leopard, macaque monkeys and gibbons at London Zoo were played alongside the film, not uncommon before the first 'talkie', *The Jazz Singer* (1927). Paramount's John Cecil Graham (second left) presented *Chang* in a sealed casket to Dr George Herbert Smith, Museum Secretary, Charles Tate Regan, Director and Dr William Calman, Keeper of Zoology. After opening the casket, as instructed, in September 1977, the film was deposited with the British Film Institute.

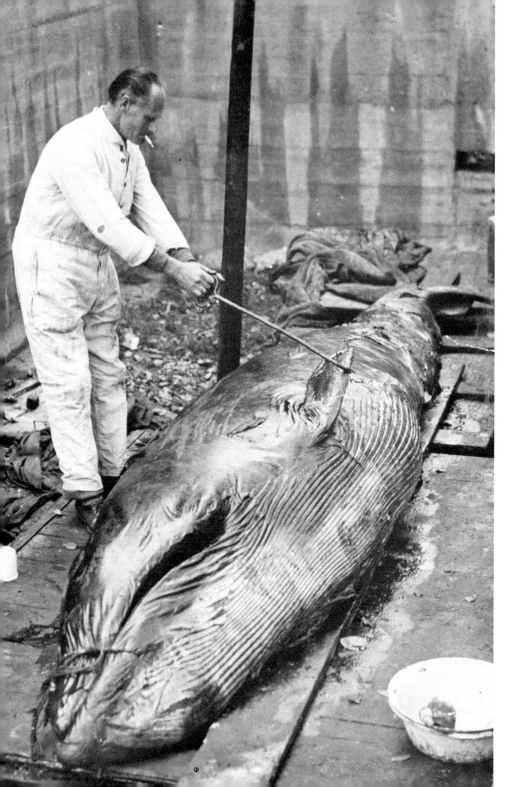

Working on whale carcass, 1930s

Since 1913, when the Crown's rights to whales and dolphins stranded or caught in English waters ('Fishes Royal') were transferred to the Museum, staff have been monitoring cetacean strandings. Several stranded minke whales, such as this one, were accessioned into the Museum collections during the 1930s. On arrival, the animal was laid out and plaster moulds were taken – fresh specimens produced the best moulds – from which plaster casts were made for display. Many of these casts still exist in the Museum's stores. The specimen was then buried to allow the oily flesh to decompose; several months later the bones were retrieved and accessioned (see p. 91).

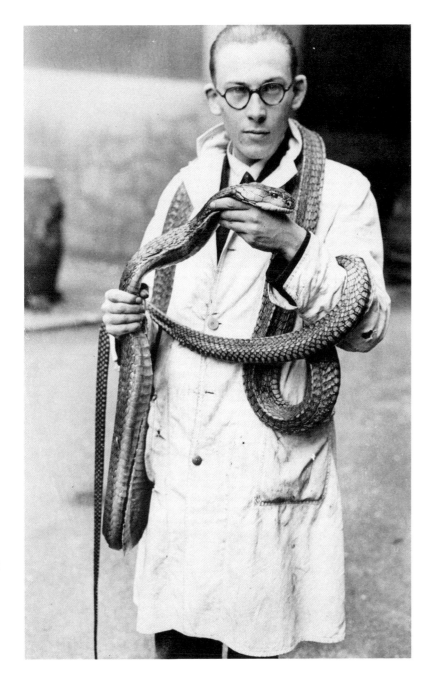

MAN WEARING SNAKE, 1930S

This bespectacled young man, possibly a junior member of the Zoology Department, is posing with a king cobra (*Ophiophagus hannah*) that presumably had just arrived at the Museum. Due to the delicate moulding of a snake's body, the complex arrangement of its scales and the natural colouration and lustre that is quickly lost, it is almost impossible to prepare a dried snake specimen to appear lifelike; most snakes on display in the Museum today are models, and the bulk of the collection is stored in spirit. Found in southeast Asia and the Philippines, as the largest of the venomous snakes, king cobras can grow up to 5 m (16 ft) long.

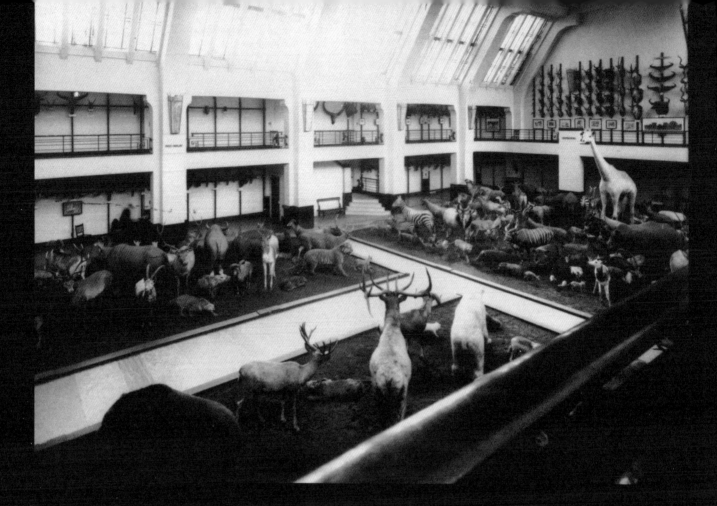

GAME ANIMALS OF THE EMPIRE EXHIBITION
AND MAN CARRYING STUFFED MAMMALS, 1932

The Game Animals of the Empire exhibition opened in the newly built Whale Hall in 1932, as finances dictated that installation of the skeletons and models of whales had to be postponed. All the specimens came from the Museum's collections except a giraffe borrowed from the taxidermists Rowland Ward Ltd. The specimens were displayed according to their place of origin, namely India, Assam, Burma, the Malay Peninsula, Borneo, Africa, Canada and Newfoundland, reminding visitors "what a very large proportion of the mammalian fauna of the world occurs within the limits of the British Empire". Captain Dollman, designer of the lighted elephant tableau in the Central Hall (see p. 76), was also responsible for arranging this exhibition.

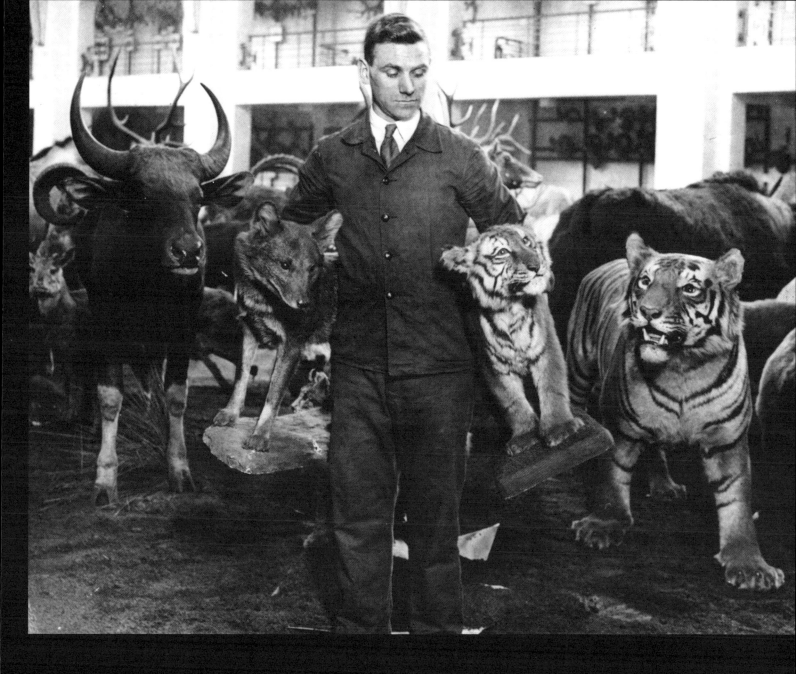

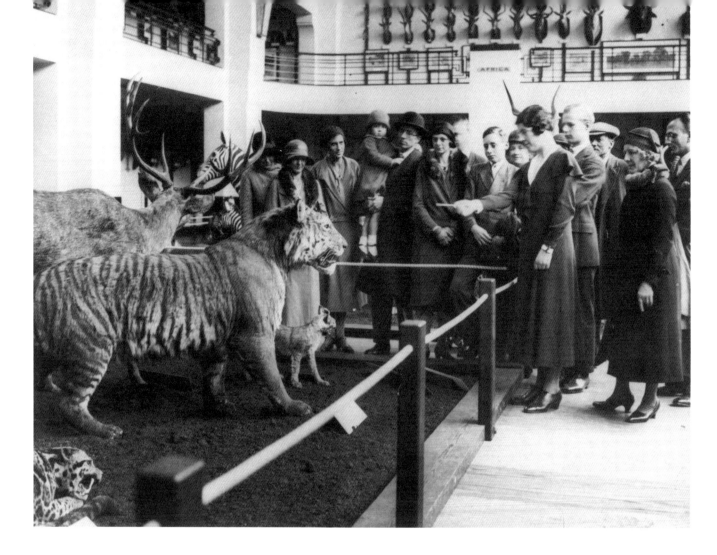

GUIDE LECTURER AT GAME ANIMALS EXHIBITION, 1932

Mona Edwards took over the job of Guide Lecturer in 1932 after the death of
John Henry Leonard. This picture shows her at work in the Game Animals of
the Empire exhibition, soon after her appointment. Although described by some
contemporaries as a "nice tyrant", the horns actually belong to an ungulate in the
Africa section behind her. A dedicated guidebook to the exhibition was also
published, providing visitors with a mass of scholarly zoological information
on the specimens displayed. Here the group is looking at a Bengal tiger in the
Indo-Malay section.

Telephonist, 1933

In 1883 the Treasury refused to sanction the Trustees' request for the purchase of telephones for the Museum, on the grounds of expense. Copper speaking tubes, as used by the Houses of Parliament, were suggested as an alternative, and can be seen behind Alfred Clayton (see p. 20). These pipes, some over 213 m (700 ft) long, ran between offices; a built-in whistle attracted the attention of the recipient (hence the phrase, being 'on the blower'), and two people could converse through the tube. It was not until 1912 that authorisation was given for a switchboard with 37 extensions and three exchange lines at a cost of £162, plus a telephonist from the Post Office to operate the system. In addition, a public call box was installed inside the main entrance.

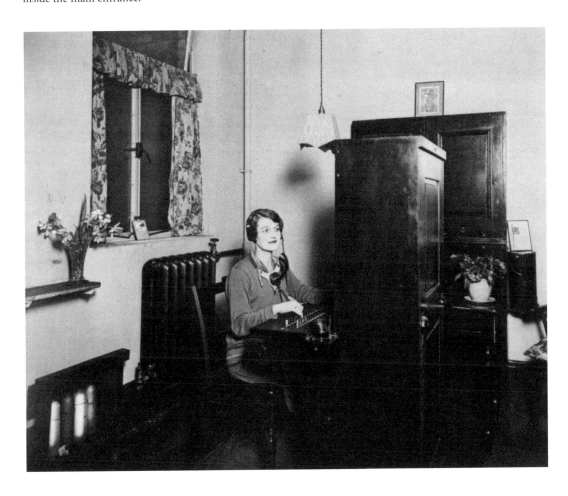

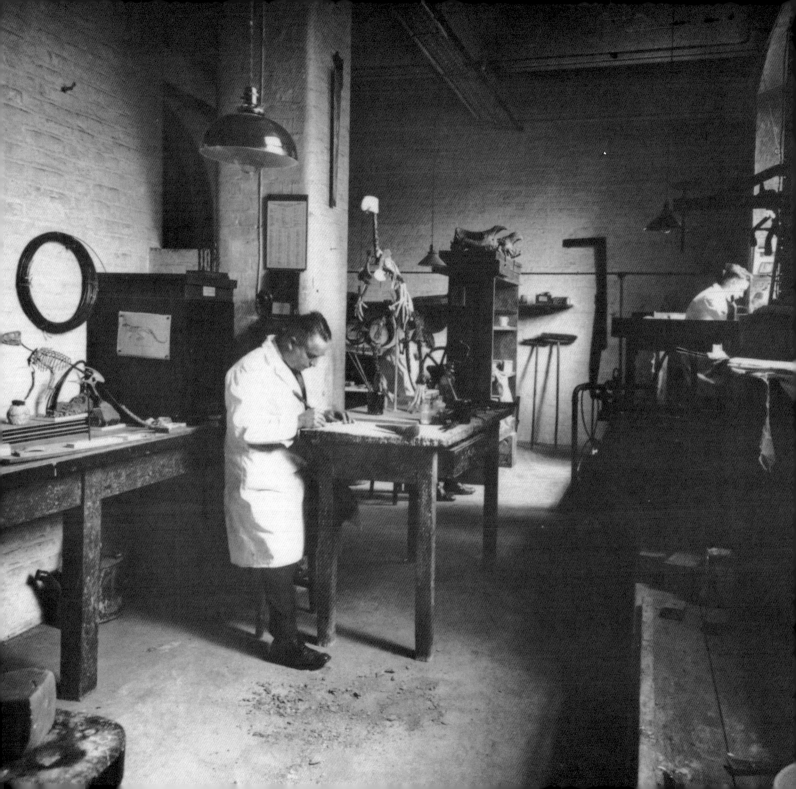

Carrying model beluga whale, c.1934

It took over a year from the closure of the old Whale Hall on 1 January 1934 for the skeletons and models, such as this dolphin, to be ready for the public in the new Whale Hall. The building was as simple as possible to avoid detracting from the exhibits. Only the ceiling was decorated, to emphasise the form of the building and to avoid a pale monotone plaster surface. A dark blue star shape was painted round two grilles in the centre of the ceiling, and a border painted around the edge. However, this was considered too distracting, and in 1938 the ceiling was painted white.

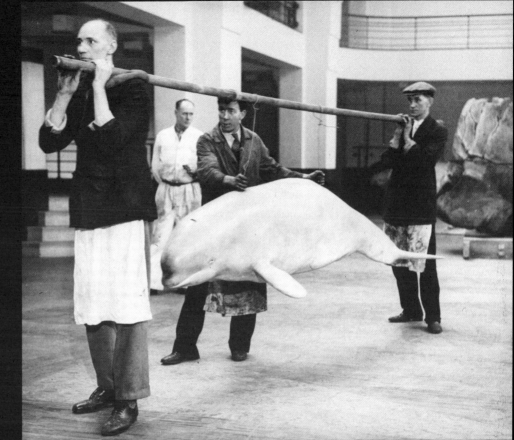

Geology Department preparators' shop, 1934

One of a series for the Museum magazine, focusing on the work that went on behind the scenes, this photograph shows Louis Parsons preparing a skeleton of the plant-eating dinosaur *Hypsilophodon* for display. Found on the Isle of Wight, and purchased by the Museum in 1924, it was originally thought to be a tree-climber and was mounted as such for exhibition. The Geology Department had two workshops in the basement of the east wing. This one dealt with the preparation of fossils and assembling the parts into specimens suitable for display or study, while the second workshop made plaster casts of natural moulds and specimens.

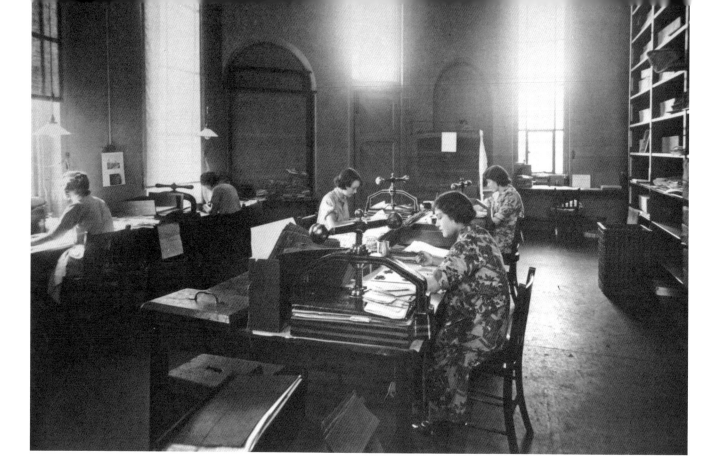

PLANT MOUNTERS, 1934

Although there were very few women on the permanent staff in the 1930s, a large number were employed as 'unofficial workers'. Five of the six plant mounters employed in the Botany Department in 1934 are shown here, in their room on the second floor of the eastern pavilion. They earned around one shilling an hour for their work, which entailed transferring specimens from the collector's temporary packaging onto herbarium sheets. The plant was gummed down and the sheet placed in the handpresses, seen here on the tables, for 24 hours. The pressed specimens were then stored in herbarium cabinets containing mothballs to help preserve the collections.

MEN IN JAWS OF BOWHEAD WHALE, 1934

In late 1934 this bowhead whale skeleton was hoisted into position in the new Whale Hall, where it still hangs today. It was a recent acquisition, from the Royal College of Surgeons, and its removal across London made the *Evening News* on 12 June 1934. The College had purchased the 14 m (46 ft) skeleton in 1864 from the Royal Zoological Museum, Copenhagen, where it had arrived the previous year from Holsteinborg, South Greenland. Bowhead whales are notable for the relative large size of their head to their body; at just over a tonne, the skull of this specimen makes up more than half the weight of the whole skeleton.

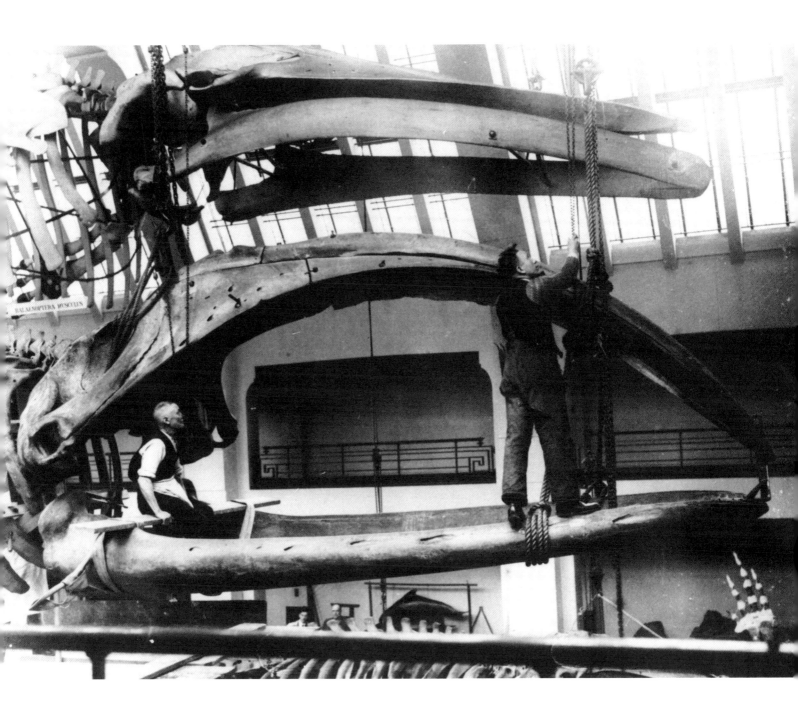

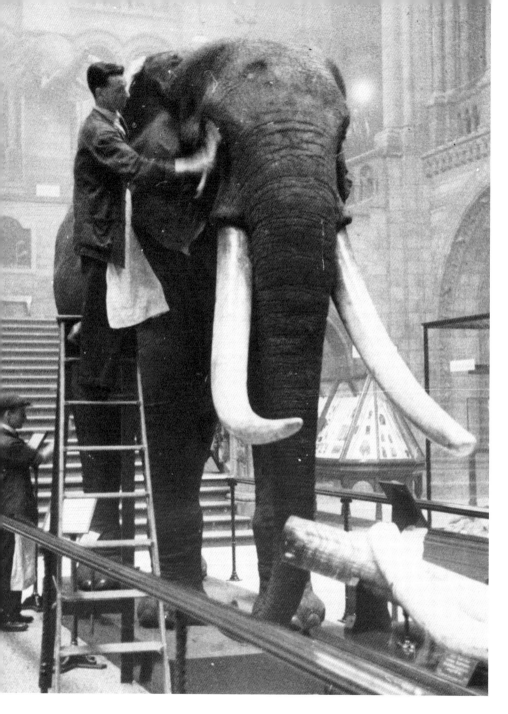

'GEORGE' THE ELEPHANT, 1935

Two attendants brush down the African elephant 'George' in the Central Hall in one of several shots of Museum staff taken by *Weekly Illustrated* photographers for an article that appeared in February 1935. Founded the previous year, this magazine exploited the new photo-reportage style of its German émigré photographers who included the editor, Stefan Lorant, as well as Felix E. Man and Bill Brandt. They were able to take sequences of slightly grainy images without reloading by using innovative Rolleiflex, Leica and Contax cameras. Lorant and Man went on to establish the famous *Picture Post* magazine in 1938.

Taxidermist working on wolf teeth, 1935

In one of several behind-the-scenes shots taken for the February 1935 edition of *Weekly Illustrated*, the final touches are added to the teeth of a wolf, *Canis lupus*. Like many of us facing a visit to the dentist, this mounted specimen just seems to grin and bear it while posing for the camera. Taxidermy and model making was undertaken by preparators, known by this time as technical assistants, attached to each of the science departments. Two years later their activities and various on-site laboratories were amalgamated to form a new, centralised Exhibition Section, under the leadership of John Doncaster who reported to the Director.

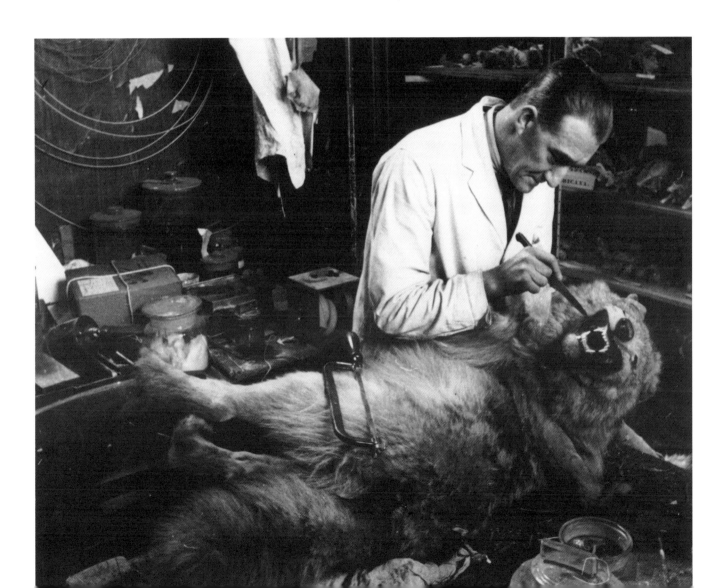

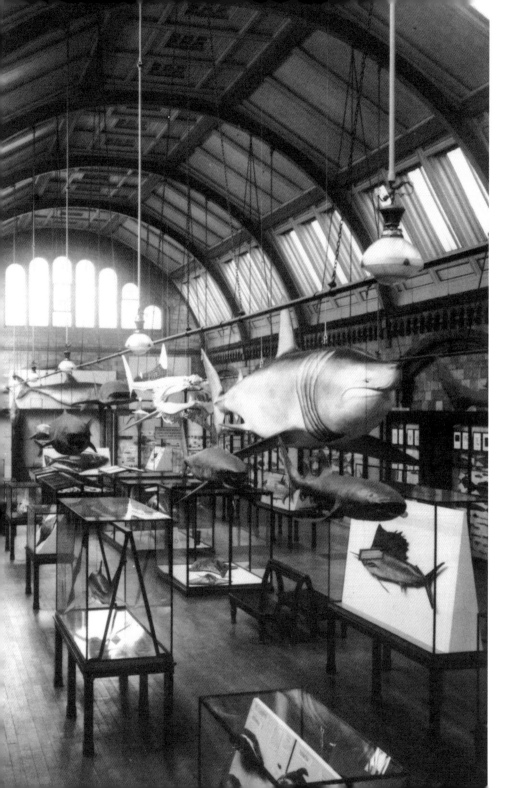

FISH GALLERY, 1935

This photograph was taken to record work-in-progress on modernising the Fish Gallery. The original displays had been set out in the early 1900s, and were arranged systematically around the walls by orders, suborders and families of fish. The new arrangement, overseen by John Norman, Assistant Keeper of Zoology, limited the classification section to the west wall cases, which were given a sky-blue background, while the rest of the gallery contained a variety of themed displays, including breeding habits, coloration, groups of fish such as poisonous, food and 'sporting' fish, and the latest scientific research relating to fisheries.

SPERM WHALE EXCAVATION, 1938

Until 1938, whale carcasses were buried in sandpits in the northwest corner of the Museum grounds (roughly where the Darwin Centre is now) to allow the flesh to rot away. This sperm whale skull and skeleton arrived in February 1937 from Bridlington, Humberside, and was duly interred. It is shown here being excavated in 1938, prior to the bones being cleaned and placed in the research collection. This 5 m (16 ft) whale was the last specimen to be given this treatment, as the burial pits were not reactivated after the war – for which the local residents were undoubtedly relieved.

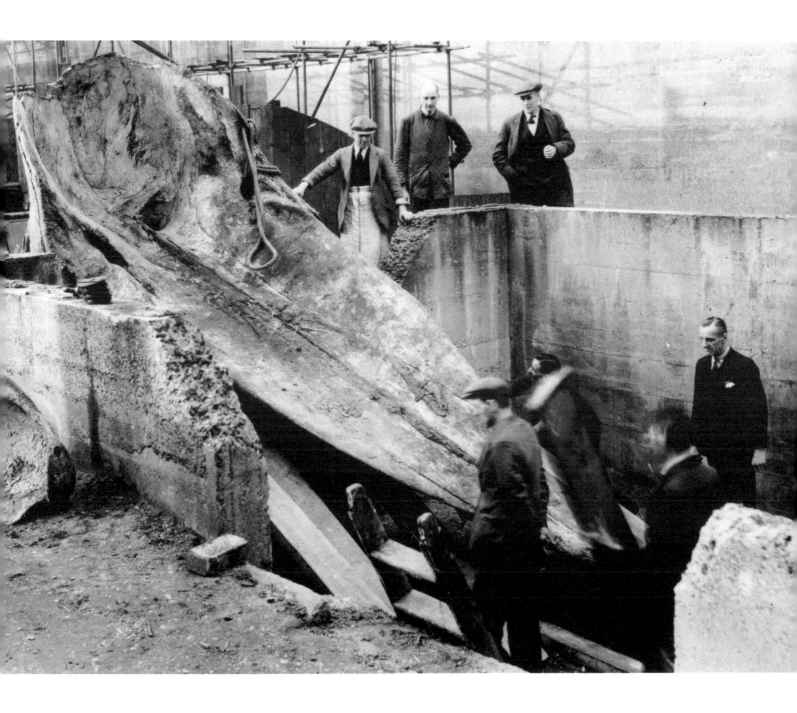

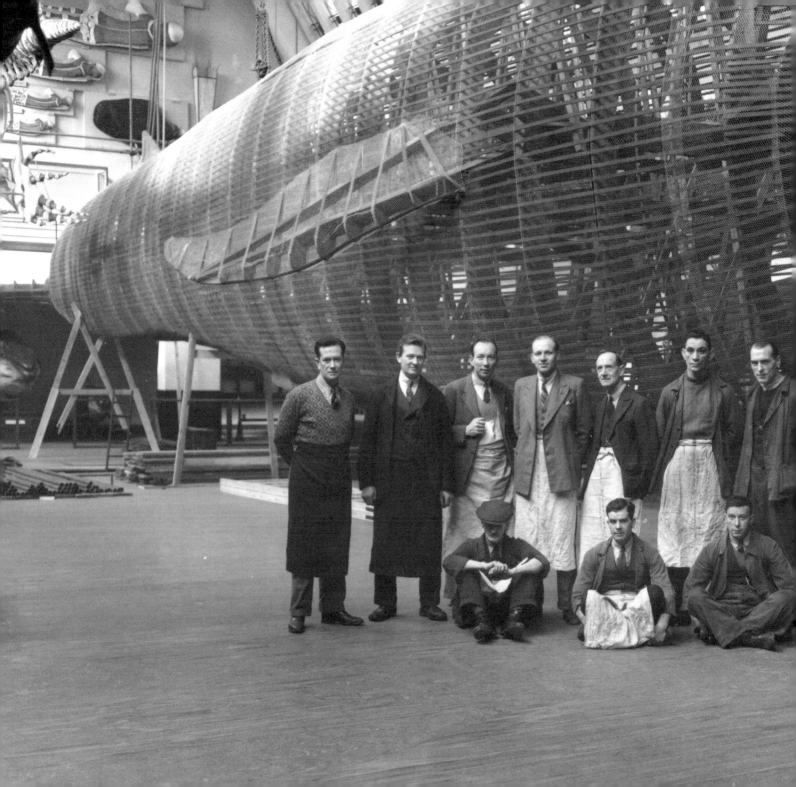

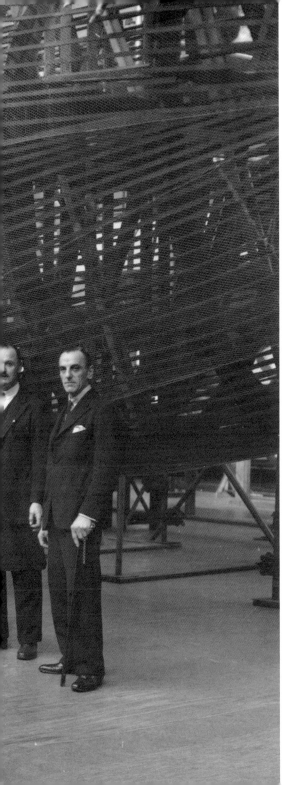

STAFF POSING WITH BLUE WHALE MODEL, JANUARY 1938

Percy and Stuart Stammwitz were part of the team that built the famous 27 m (90 ft) blue whale model. The public was disappointed that the new Whale Hall did not contain the models that the old Hall had done, so it was decided to build a new model that would be the envy of other museums. A 229 cm (90 in) long scale model was made in January 1936, based on measurements and photos of a series of whales caught in Antarctic waters. Work on the full-size model began in mid-1937, shown here in January 1938 with the joiners who built the wooden framework.

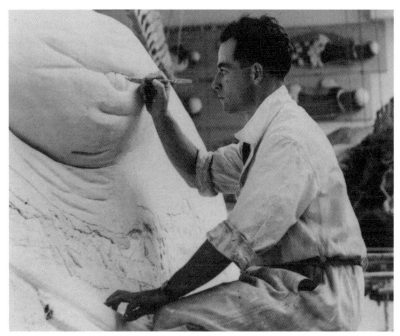

STUART STAMMWITZ WORKING ON BLUE WHALE MODEL, 1938

The preparators dispensed with the usual time-consuming procedures of taking casts and moulds which were subsequently destroyed. A wooden framework, built in situ in the Whale Hall, was covered by a light expanding metal, and plaster was applied directly onto the frame. Stuart Stammwitz is shown here working on the whale's eye, before the model was painted. The flippers of the skeletons hanging above the new installation had to be raised as they obscured the view of the model, but it was finally ready in December 1938. References to a time capsule in the belly of the whale have never been verified.

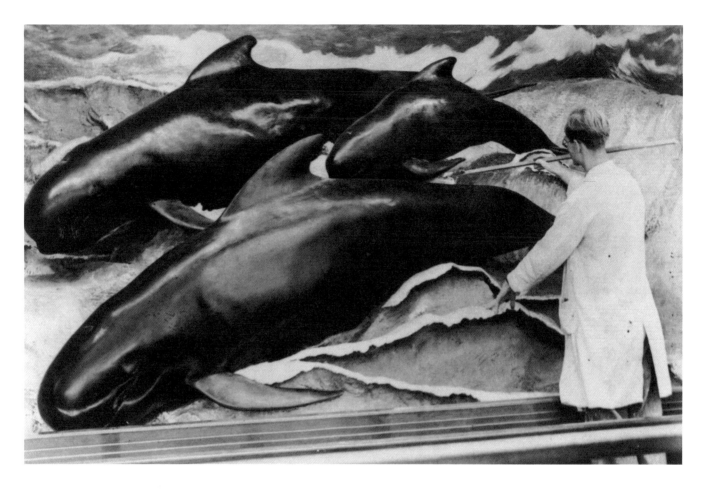

David Macer-Wright painting pilot whale exhibit, 1938

David Macer-Wright hoped for many years to work at the Museum, and his wish was finally fulfilled in July 1937 when he was employed for exhibition work, attached to the Zoology Department. His first year coincided with the preparation of the blue whale model and the completion of the Whale Hall displays, and much of his work consisted of assisting Percy and Stuart Stammwitz, besides completing a considerable number of other pieces of plasterwork and models. Macer-Wright's tasks included printing the labels for the dolphin and whale casts in the Hall, and assisting with the preparation of the pilot whale exhibit, which he can be seen painting here.

OPEN CASE WITH SNAKE SKELETON, 1939

This Indian python skeleton, *Python molurus*, is still on display today. It was probably acquired around 1900 for exhibition in the Reptile Gallery (the Museum's collections were divided into exhibition specimens and study collections), possibly from a zoo. The character of the Reptile Gallery changed very little between the 1880s and the 1970s, when, with the Crustacea and Fish Galleries at the rear of the west wing, it was redeveloped as part of the New Exhibition Scheme to create the Hall of Human Biology. The reptiles remaining on display were moved to a new home off the North Hall.

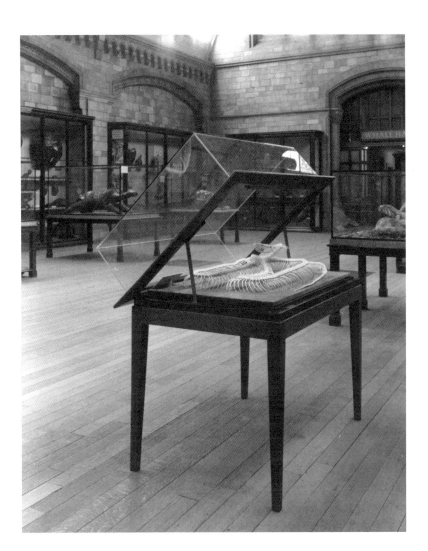

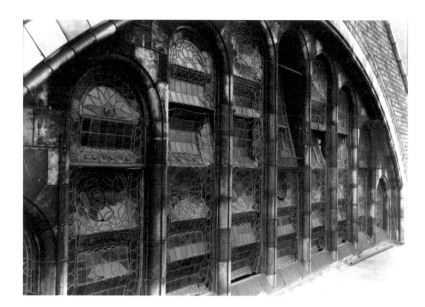

DAMAGED WINDOWS, 1940

Between September 1940 and April 1941 the Museum suffered several bad air raids, after which there was a lull until the flying bombs, the 'doodlebugs', of 1944. By the end of the war, almost every window and glass exhibit case in the Museum had been broken, and due to glass shortages it was a number of years before the building was restored to its former glory.

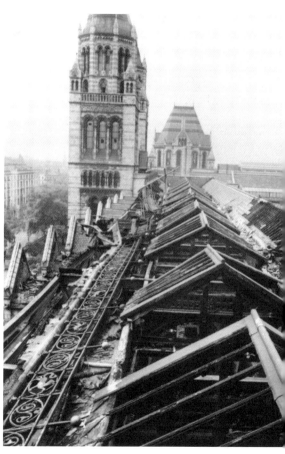

DAMAGED ROOF OF BOTANY DEPARTMENT, 1940

At 4.30 a.m. on 9 September 1940, two incendiaries and an oil bomb, jettisoned by a German bomber, hit the roof of the Botany Department in the east wing. The top floor housing the General Herbarium was severely damaged by the fire and many specimens and books were destroyed. The construction of the roof contributed to its own destruction – it contained a series of inaccessible tunnels which acted as flues when a bomb hit the end of one of them. Notably, however, water used to extinguish the fires caused the surprise germination of some Chinese lotus seeds collected in 1793.

Damage in Shell Gallery, 1940

Another serious air raid occurred just over a month after the General Herbarium was hit, on the night of 16 October 1940. An incendiary bomb hit the Shell Gallery (now the Jerwood Gallery), seriously damaging the roof and causing a major fire which proved difficult to tackle. The damage was substantial, and a great deal of water used to extinguish the flames flooded into the Osteological basement below. Temporary repairs were carried out, but in 1947, when the gallery was converted into a lecture hall, the walls still needed cleaning.

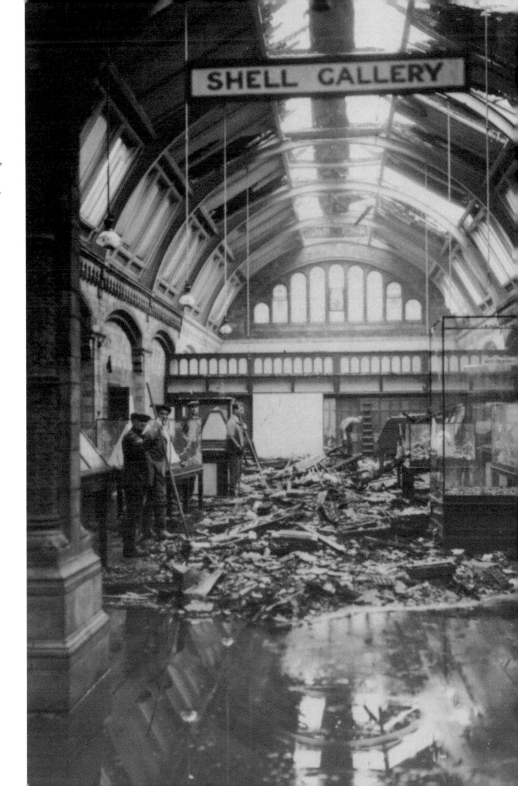

LOOKING FOR SHRAPNEL, 1940

Appearing in a series of photographs jokingly entitled 'Soter & Hetaerus' ('saviour' and 'companion' in Greek), these two men are Arthur Hopwood, Assistant Keeper of Geology, appointed Salvage Officer in 1940, and Clive Forster Cooper, Director of the Museum. The Salvage Officer's remit – part of a national drive to collect anything that could be of use for the war effort – included collecting scrap iron, and the two men apparently went round the Museum collecting pieces of shrapnel after bombing raids. In July 1940 it was reported that scrap metal to the value of £3 15s had been sold off to the Kensington Salvage Department.

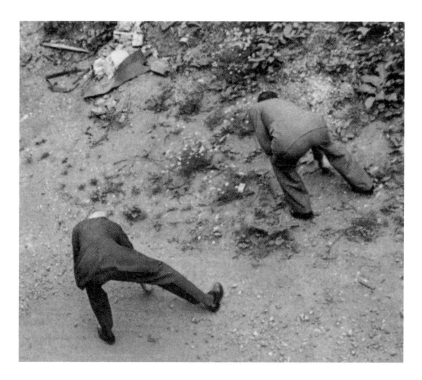

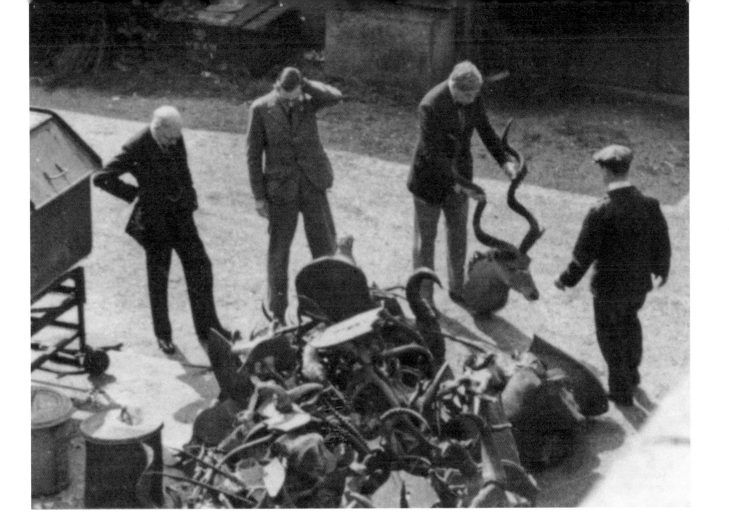

MEN WITH HORNED SPECIMENS, 1940

This photograph, together with the photograph on p. 98, appeared in the August 1940 edition of *Tin Hat*, the anonymous and very unofficial bulletin that was produced on various Museum typewriters between 1939 and 1942. It was edited by the Librarian, Alexander Townsend, a Greek scholar and therefore probably the source of the pseudonyms 'Soter' and 'Hetaerus'. The scrap iron salvage scheme included such items as old typewriters and, from this picture, possibly the metal hangings from the mounted antelope heads. Hopwood's assiduity in his role was mocked gently in *Tin Hat*, which pointed out that he had not yet collected all the Museum keys and the hooks on which they hung.

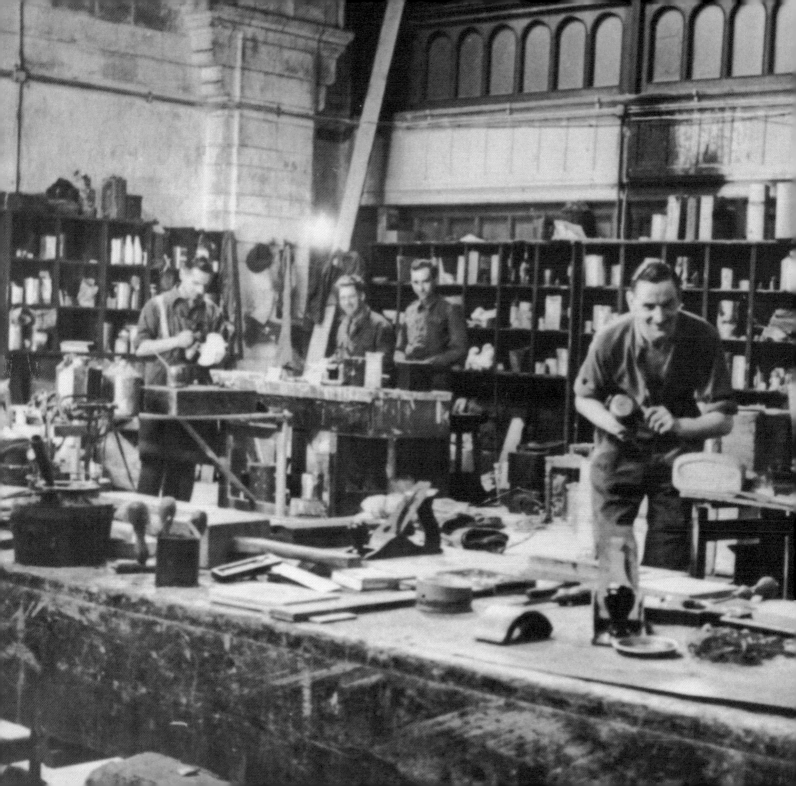

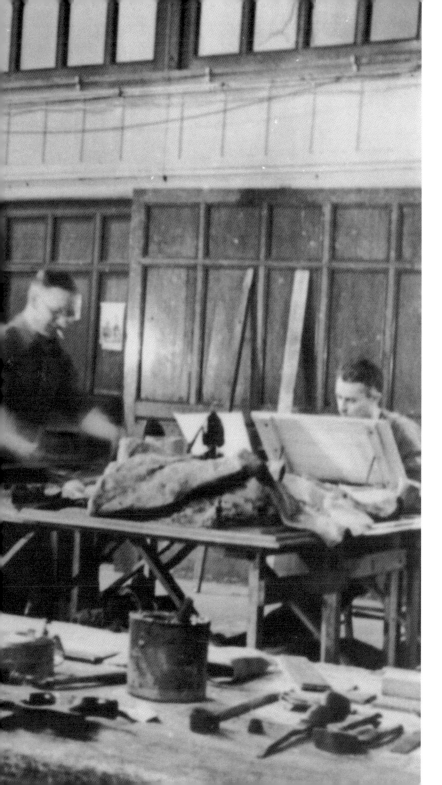

SOE CRAFTSMEN, C. 1943

The Special Operations Executive (SOE) was formed in 1940 as a secret service under the aegis of the Minister of Economic Warfare. Under the cover name of the Inter-Services Research Bureau, its mission was "to aid and encourage all resistance to the enemy in occupied territories". Three galleries and part of a corridor at the western end of the Museum were assigned to the SOE's Camouflage Section for their top-secret Demonstration Room, designated Station XVb. The area at the north end of what is now the Jerwood Gallery was fitted out as a workshop for the plasterers and carpenters involved in preparing materials for agents in the field.

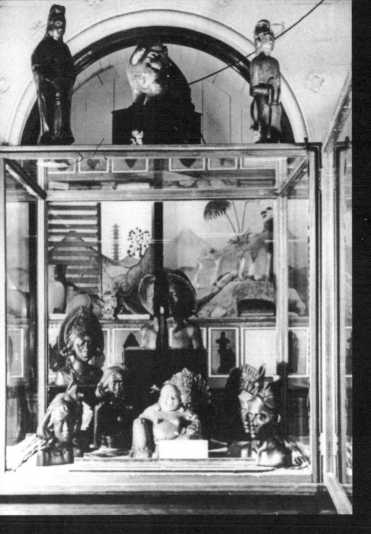

High-explosive carvings, c. 1943

The SOE craftsmen had to provide materials for agents all over the world. These innocent-looking Oriental carvings are in fact cast in solid high explosive, coloured to represent wood, sandstone or porcelain, and designed to be detonated by time delay. The War Office produced top-secret catalogues of such devices, explaining that local agents in the Far East would pose as hawkers on the quaysides and sell the carvings to Japanese troops about to embark.

Incendiary and Demolition Charges Hall, c. 1943

This room was used to show agents what sabotage tools they could use behind enemy lines. Among the devices created by the plasterers in the workshop was imitation coal to be filled with explosive, dummy logs in which munitions could be hidden, and ball and skittle sets, which hid hand grenades in the skittles and a detonator in the ball. Perhaps one of the most memorable exhibits on display in the Demonstration Room was the explosive rat – literally a skin filled with explosive and a detonator.

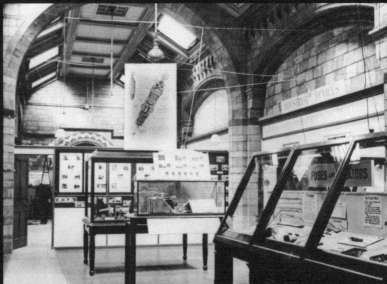

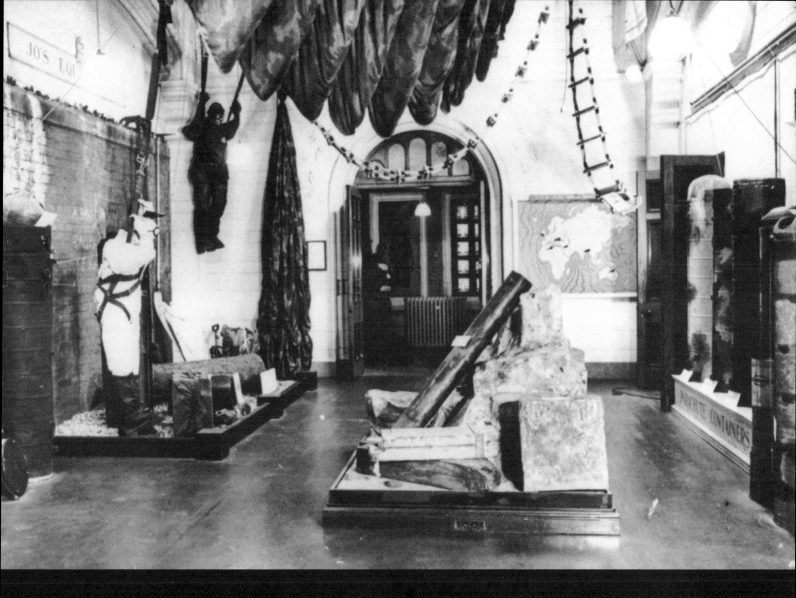

MILITARY DISPLAY, C. 1943

The Demonstration Room showcased practically everything an SOE agent would need to operate effectively. Partly designed to inform the agents about what was available and to inspire them with ideas, senior British and Allied officials and VIPs – including George VI – were also brought here to be briefed about the SOE and its capabilities.

BIRD GALLERY, 1944

The Bird Gallery was located on the ground floor in the west wing. On 11 July 1944 a flying bomb landed in Cromwell Road and all the glass in the west wing, inside and out, was broken. A section of the iron railings was found in the Bird Gallery, and a red-necked pharolope, mounted in a flying position, was sucked out of the building with the rush of air after the blast. A report notes, however, that its "homing instinct was too strong and it was ultimately found on a table in the Entomological basement below".

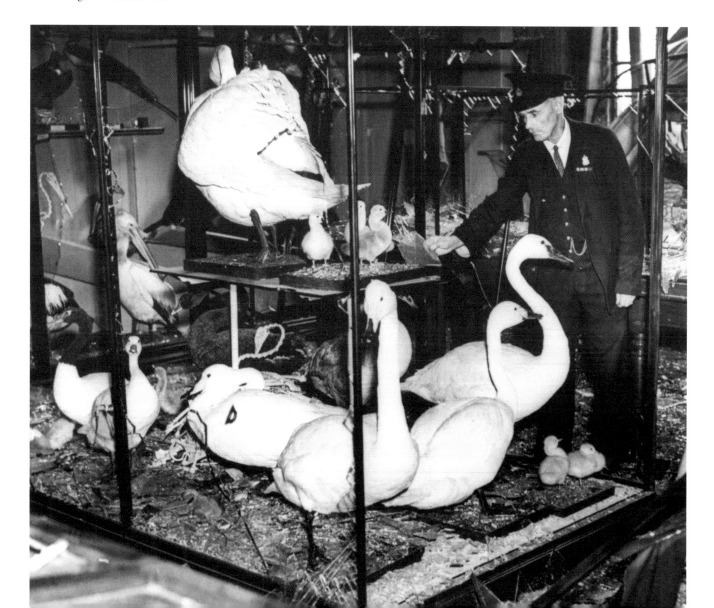

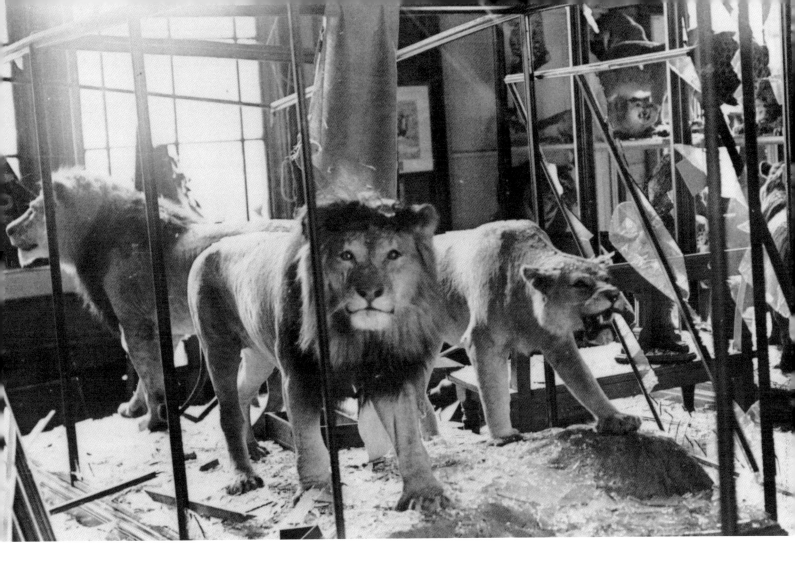

LIONS IN DEBRIS, 1944

The flying bomb of 11 July 1944 followed one on 5 July, and together the two did a great deal of damage, as can be seen here in the Lower Mammal Gallery. Some 1465 sheets of glass were broken in the Mammal Galleries alone, showering the exhibits with dust and glass shards which lodged in the coats of the long-haired animals and cut the short-haired specimens. Skylights in the Central and North Halls, the Whale Hall at the rear of the Museum, and the back galleries, some of which had just been repaired, were also broken.

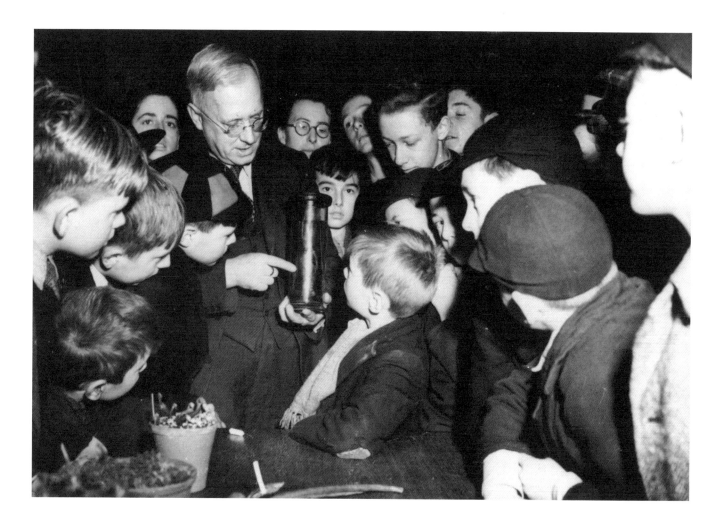

CHILDREN AROUND SIR JOHN RAMSBOTTOM WITH SPIRIT JAR,
DECEMBER 1948

From 28 December 1948 to 11 January 1949, a series of lectures with a difference
were held at the Museum. At 2.15 p.m. every weekday, a member of one of the
science departments imparted his knowledge to an eager audience of schoolchildren
in the former Shell Gallery. Illustrated by films, slides and specimens, the lectures
were quite informal and often took the form of question and answer sessions. Total
attendance was 1656, prompting the Museum to consider making it a more regular
occurrence. The scientist here is Sir John Ramsbottom, Keeper of Botany, 1930-50.

Children with bird specimens, 1948

In December 1948 a Children's Centre opened at the Museum. Jacqueline Palmer, a teacher seconded from the London County Council, had come up with the idea after noticing that many children wandered aimlessly around the Museum, gaining little benefit from their visit. One of the bays on the west side of the Central Hall was set aside for the purpose, and treasure hunts, competitions and games were organised. Unusual specimens could be brought along for identification, and children could obtain pencil and paper to draw their favourite specimen, either in the Centre, as these two are doing, or out in the galleries.

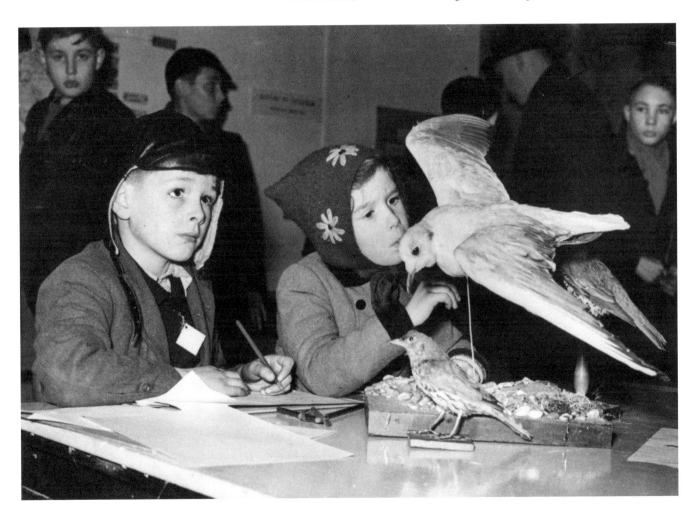

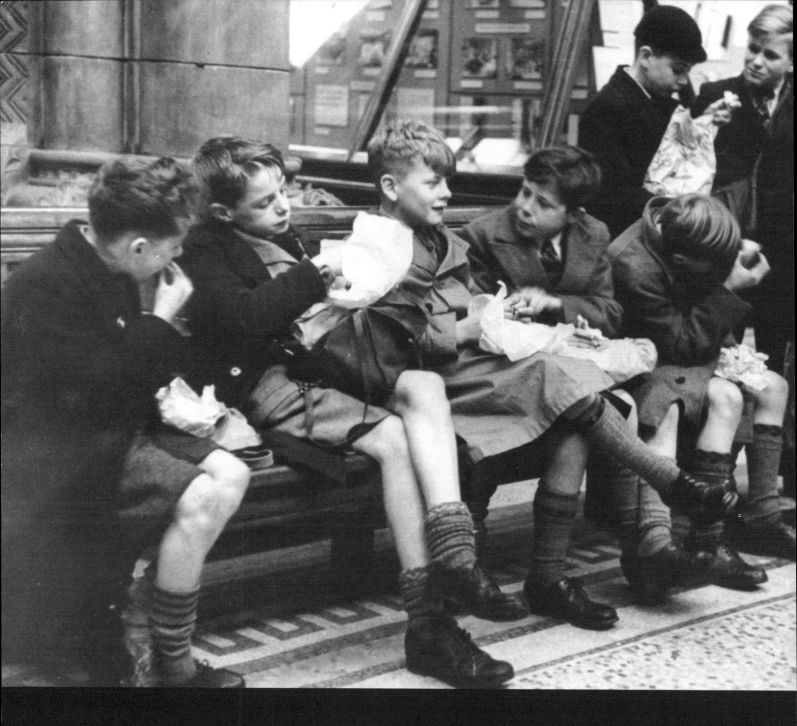

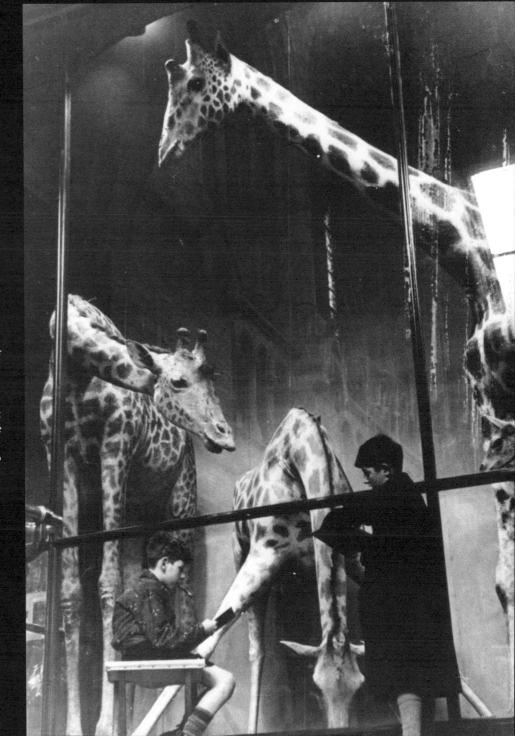

BOYS PICNICKING, 1948

These boys appear to be on a school trip (incidentally breaking the rule of no eating in the public galleries), and would probably have visited the Children's Centre. The Centre was partially intended to make up for the lack of natural history teaching in the classroom, besides encouraging children to use the Museum intelligently and to relate what they saw to the world around them. Jacqueline Palmer, who ran the Children's Centre, recognised that many children had a latent interest in natural history which could be brought out. Through fun activities, she aimed to educate the children who flocked to the Centre during the holidays – numbers had to be limited due to high demand – and even returned on Saturdays during term.

BOYS SKETCHING GIRAFFES, 1949

For the really keen juvenile naturalist aged between ten and fifteen, a Junior Naturalists' Club was established. Entry was gained by producing a piece of fieldwork to prove one's dedication to the study of natural history, and club members had a room and library of their own to use on Saturdays. But it was a serious business – in June 1950 six members were 'sent down', back to the Children's Centre, as a result of the periodic review of work that the Club insisted upon to maintain standards. In 1953 a Field Observers' Club was established for young people over fifteen; both clubs were later affiliated to external organisations.

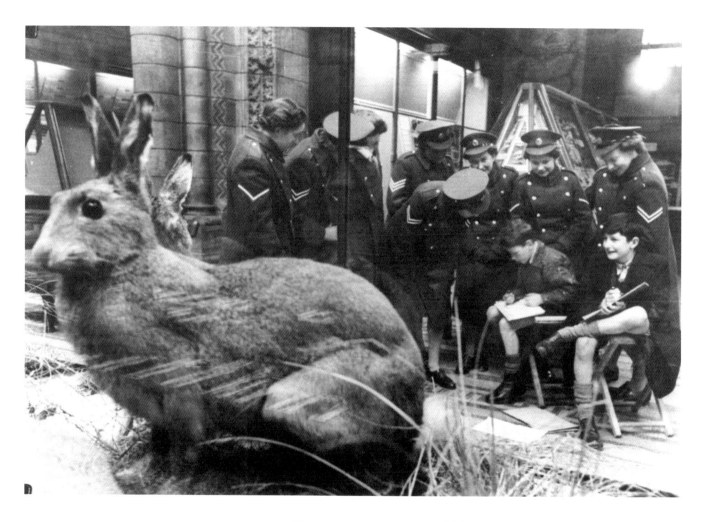

Boys sketching rabbit, 1949

To ensure the children actually learnt something, they had to research and produce a description of the animals they drew. Information sheets and specimens that could be handled were available in the Centre for this purpose. Field trips were organised in the Museum grounds and at other suitable locations. The Children's Centre provoked a certain amount of interest in the newspapers, and in May 1949 the Museum hosted a conference on 'Children in Museums'. The boys' work is being admired by a group from the Women's Royal Auxiliary Corps: a sergeant, corporals and lance corporals serving with the Royal Military Police.

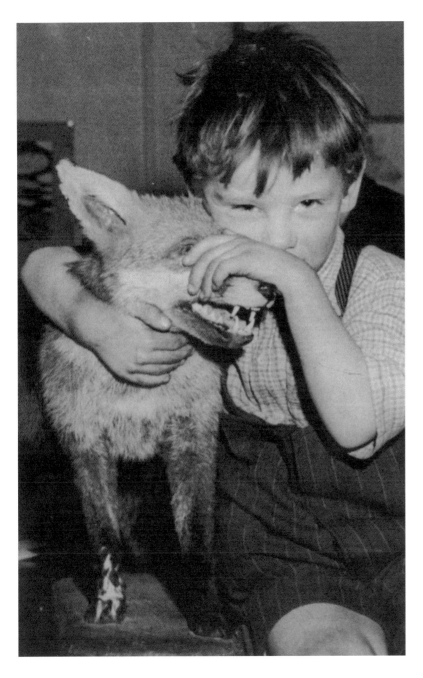

LITTLE BOY WITH FOX, C. 1950

Parents and older siblings were actively discouraged from visiting the Children's Centre, to ensure that the children were free to be themselves. This little boy is probably among the youngest of the attendees, but many of the children kept up their involvement for a number of years – photographs taken during the course of the 1950s show some of the same individuals as they grow up.

ACKNOWLEDGEMENTS

We have attempted to check all details in the captions but any accidental errors in the text are our own. We would like to thank all those who helped us by providing additional information. In particular we would like to acknowledge the contribution of various Museum colleagues: the Publishing team and staff in our Photo Unit; Alison Harding and Lorraine Portch, Library and Information Services; Jennifer Bryant, Botany; Andy Currant, Sandra Chapman and Angela Milner and Pip Brewer, Palaeontology; Paul Clark, Daphne Hills, Paula Jenkins, Colin McCarthy and Richard Sabin, Zoology; Eric Groves and Robert Ross, Scientific Associates, and Keith Hyatt, retired zoologist. We have also received invaluable help from many others, including: Christopher Date and Gary Thorn at the British Museum; Kate Pickard and Claire Daniel at the Royal Botanic Gardens, Kew; Sue Breakell, Nigel Steel and Diana Condell at the Imperial War Museum; The Royal Archives, Windsor; Simon Moody at the National Army Museum; the Zoological Society of London Library; the National Portrait Gallery; Bernadette Callery at the Carnegie Museum of Natural History; Professor Pietro Passerin d'Entrèves, Director, SUISM, Università degli Studi di Torino; and Charlotte and Mrs Priscilla Manley.

Note
It has been possible to identify many former members of staff in the photographs, but we welcome any help with naming those who remain anonymous. We are always keen to obtain additional items or to take the opportunity to copy images to enhance our holdings. Visitors are welcome to look at images in the collection by appointment.

Susan Snell and Polly Parry
www.nhm.ac.uk/library/archives/

PICTURE CREDITS

Every effort has been made to contact and accurately credit all copyright holders. If we have been unsuccessful, we apologise and welcome corrections for future editions or reprints.

p.24, Scientists at play, 1899, by kind permission of Mrs P Manley, daughter of R H Bunting

p.26, Botany staff, March 1900, by kind permission of Mrs P Manley, daughter of R H Bunting

p.30, Taxidermists at work, 1902, published by Cassell & Co.

p.40, African elephant in Central Hall, February 1910, Clarke & Hyde Press Agency

p.46, Bengal tiger, 1913, © The Sport & General Press Agency

p.58, A Wealden mollusc, 1924, Special Press

p.73, Children examining tiger, c. 1927, © Associated Newspapers

p.75, Darwin statue, September 1927, © Associated Newspapers

p.89, Taxidermist working on wolf teeth, 1935, Weekly Illustrated

p.90, 'George' the elephant, 1935, Weekly Illustrated

p.93 right, Stuart Stammwitz working on blue whale model, 1938, MC Photos

p.94, David Macer-Wright painting pilot whale exhibit, 1938, MC Photos

pp.100–101, SOE Craftsmen, c. 1943, © Imperial War Museum, HU61060

p.102 left, High-explosive carvings, c. 1943, © Imperial War Museum, HU61175

p.102 right, Incendiary and Demolition Charges Hall, c. 1943, © Imperial War Museum, HU61069

p.103, Military display, c. 1943, © Imperial War Museum, HU61115

p.104, Bird Gallery, 1944, © Associated Newspapers

p.105, Lions in debris, 1944, © Associated Newspapers

p.107, Children with bird specimens, 1948, © The Sport & General Press Agency

p.108, Boys picnicking, 1948, © popperfoto.com

p.109, Boys sketching giraffes, 1949, © popperfoto.com

p.110, Boys sketching rabbit, 1949, © popperfoto.com

All other images are copyright of the Natural History Museum. For copies of these and other images, view the online Picture Library at www.nhm.ac.uk/piclib, or contact them directly at the Natural History Museum.